Bob Black

ANARCHY AFTER LEFTISM

First edited by C. A. L. Press, 1997.

Present edition by Lothric Wildman, 2023.

Retrived from *theanarchistlibrary.org*

ISBN : 978-1-4478-7833-9

Bob Black

Anarchy after Leftism

A Farewell to the Anarchism That Was !

Edited by
Lothric Wildman
2023

« Anarchy will not be vital until the last leftist is hung with the guts of the last Social Ecologist »

- Paul Z. Simons

« Traditional or classical anarchism is as outmoded as the rest of the Left. It is not at all part of the oft-noticed surge of interest in Anarchy. Note the usage here: it isn't anarchism that is moving forward, but Anarchy. Not a closed, Eurocentric ideology but an open, no-holds-barred questioning and resisting »

- John Zerzan

Bob Black

ANARCHY AFTER LEFTISM

TABLE OF CONTENTS

Preface *by Jason McQuinn* .7

Introduction .11

Chapter 1: Murray Bookchin, Grumpy Old Man .15

Chapter 2: What is Individualist Anarchism? .25

Chapter 3: Lifestyle Anarchism .40

Chapter 4: On Organization .47

Chapter 5: Murray Bookchin, Municipal Statist .60

Chapter 6: Reason and Revolution .69

Chapter 7: In Search of the Primitivists Part I: Pristine Angles .80

Chapter 8: In Search of the Primitivists Part II: Primitive Affluence .96

Chapter 9: From Primitive Affluence to Labor-Enslaving Technology .101

Chapter 10: Shut Up, Marxist! .108

Chapter 11: Anarchy after Leftism .109

References .119

APPENDIX :

What Left and Right really Mean *by Bellamy Fitzpatrick* .137

Bob Black

Preface

Leaving the twentieth century, leftism of every stripe is in disarray and defeat — anarcho-leftism included. And Murray Bookchin's Social Ecology is certainly no exception to this trend.

Bookchin, one of the best known of contemporary North American anarchists, has spent much of his life staking out his own personal eco-anarchist ideological territory under the banners of Social Ecology and Libertarian Municipalism. He is the author of a steady stream of books from the sixties to the present, including his classic collection of essays titled *Post-Scarcity Anarchism* published in 1971, his excellent volume on the history of the Spanish anarchist movement written in the seventies, and his failed attempt in the eighties at constructing a philosophical magnum opus in *The Ecology of Freedom.*

Bookchin has never been content with merely constructing one more radical ideology in competition with all the others. His dream has always been to lead a coherent left-wing ecological radical grouping into a serious contest with the powers that be. However, his attempts at constructing such a grouping (from the *Anarchos* journal group in the New York of the sixties to the recent Left Green Network within the Greens milieu) have never met with much success.

In his latest book, *Social Anarchism or Lifestyle Anarchism,* Bookchin aims to pin the blame for his lifetime of frustration (despite his decades of valiant effort!) on an evil anti-socialist conspiracy which has subverted his dreams at every turn: the dreaded specter of "Lifestyle Anarchism." For Bookchin, lifestyle anarchism is a contemporary manifestation of the individualist anarchist currents which have always bedeviled the world anarchist movement proper. The fact that the anarchist "movement" itself has always been more of a polymorphous insurrectionary *milieu* encompassing everything from anarcho-syndicalists, anarcho-communists and anarcho-futurists to anarchist feminists, anarchist primitivists and anarcho-situationists doesn't really matter to him. The important thing is that he has finally been able to name the anti-organizational cabal which opposes him and to explain the esoteric links between its often seemingly unrelated or even mutually contradictory efforts!

Enter Bob Black.

Now a lot of people don't like Bob Black. Many *anarchists* would be alarmed if he moved in next door. Anyone with good sense would probably be upset if he started dating her younger sister. Most everyone is loathe to provoke his anger or face it head on.

And not without reason. Bob may be a brilliant critic and hilarious wit, but he's not a nice guy. His infamous reputation isn't built on fair play or good sportsmanship.

Maybe this is why Murray Bookchin's latest rant, *Social Anarchism or Lifestyle Anarchism: An Unbridgeable Chasm,* never criticizes Bob Black directly. In fact it never so much as mentions Bob's name. Even though it's obvious from the book's contents that by all rights Bob should have received the same type of attempted (though ultimately feeble) thrashing Bookchin reserved for George Bradford, John Zerzan, Hakim Bey, *et al.*

Obviously, Murray knows better than to challenge Bob to a duel, even a *rhetorical* one. But that hasn't stopped Bob, in an uncharacteristically generous spirit, from giving Bookchin his due *anyway.*

Bob's defense of anarchy in *Anarchy after Leftism* isn't meant to express solidarity with those targeted in the latest attacks framed by Bookchin's pidgin dialectics. Nor is Bob really interested in rescuing anarchist ideology from itself. He just wants to set the record straight by clearing away worse than useless polemics. Defending the potential for anarchy is merely an unpleasant task of menial anti-ideological labor that Bob has performed because no one else volunteered to wash these particular dirty dishes,[1] while he wants to get on with cooking another meal.

---

[1] The *Fifth Estate's* David Watson (aka George Bradford) *has* just written a valuable critique of major themes in Bookchin's work titled *Beyond Bookchin:*

But that's by no means all that's going on here. Disposing of Murray Bookchin's ideological and rhetorical rubbish gives Bob the chance to develop the grounds for a more general attack on the remaining vestiges of leftism while he's at it. Cleaning house of leftism is a much bigger task than dealing with one man's leftist career. So in one sense, by drawing attention to his ineffectual polemic, Bookchin has made himself an excuse for the beginning of a much larger process of critique, a process that will undoubtedly continue to unfold with increasing militance into the coming century. It will require awareness and effort from all of us to finish this task, but it *will* be done.

Bob's double critique in *Anarchy after Leftism* only gains incisiveness from the attitude of lumpen *noblesse oblige* he has adopted for his task. Rather than letting his own sordid past (and present) get in the way, the lack of any revenge motive (seemingly Bob's favorite muse) allows him to unleash his pen with just as much wit, but with fewer red herrings, obscure put-downs and tortured self-justifications than ever. The result is a modest feast made up of consistently entertaining prose, an immanent critique of a would-be eminent social critic, and one more nail in the coffin of obsolete leftism, anarchist-style.

You might not want to invite Bob into your house. I certainly wouldn't. But at least thank him for doing the dishes. And let's get on with the next feast!

Jason McQuinn

Anarchy: A Journal of Desire Armed

Alternative Press Review

Preface for a Future Social Ecology, published by Autonomedia (Brooklyn, NY) and Black & Red (Detroit, MI). It was also stimulated by Bookchin's abysmal *Social Anarchism or Lifestyle Anarchism.* However, Watson's work is aimed more towards defending anarcho-primitivism and rehabilitating a non-Bookchinist Social Ecology than towards the critique Bob takes on in this volume of Bookchin's leftover leftism served in biodegradable ecological and municipalist wrappings.

Bob Black

Introduction

This small book is nothing more than a critique of another small book, Murray Bookchin's *Social Anarchism or Lifestyle Anarchism: An Unbridgeable Chasm*.[2] His consists of the title essay plus "The Left That Was: A Personal Reflection." Published in 1995, it was an unexpected intervention in an intramural debate which had been going on for at least twenty years between traditionalistic anarchists — leftist, workerist, organizational, and moralist — and an ever more diverse (and an ever more numerous) contingent of anarchists who

---

[2] Edinburgh, Scotland & San Francisco, CA: AK Press, 1995. All references consisting solely of numerals in parentheses are page references to this book. All other references — be they to Bookchin's other writings or the writings of others — follow an approximation of social-science citation style. That is, they consist of a parenthetical reference to a source by the last name of the author and the year of publication followed by, in some instances, specific page references. For example, (Black 1994: 50) refers to page 50 of the book listed in the Bibliography as follows:

Black, Bob (1994). *Beneath the Underground*. Portland, OR: Feral House & Port Townsend, WA: Loompanics Unlimited

Sometimes the author's name is omitted if, in context, it is provided or implied in the text, *e.g.*, (1994: 50) where the text itself has identified Black as the source.

I request the forbearance of readers who think that in explaining the almost-obvious I am talking down to them. I expect that nearly all of my readers are either familiar with this citation system or else would have no difficulty figuring it out. I chose to use it to supply at least the rudiments of references simultaneously with what I make of them. I choose to explain the system here from an excess of caution.

I expect the Bookchinist counterattack to rely heavily on confusionist quibbling about details, including bibliographic details. Some anarchists are unduly impressed by the trappings of scholarship, unaware that, if carefully scrutinized, they are sometimes only claptrappings. Some are even susceptible to typeset text as such, as if typesetting were some sort of guarantee that the text is presumptively important and/or true.

To a considerable extent, Bookchin's seeming scholarship is shallow or sham, and that's especially true of *Social Anarchism or Lifestyle Anarchism*. To demonstrate that, as this essay does, my scholarship will have to be much better and much more honest. Careful referencing, and a clear understanding of my method of referencing, is crucial to that demonstration. For you, gentle reader, the worst is now behind you. Let the games begin!

have in one way or another departed from orthodoxy, at least in Bookchin's eyes.

Bookchin caught a lot of us heterodox anarchists by surprise. Most of us have read some of Bookchin's books and many of us, myself included, have learned from them, especially the earlier books from the 1970s. Bookchin's subsequent and ever-intensifying preoccupation with municipal politics we were mostly inclined to ignore as an idiosyncrasy. He seemed to take no notice of what *we* were up to. He was absent from publications like the *Fifth Estate, Popular Reality, Front Line, The Match!,* and *Anarchy: A Journal of Desire Armed.* It was as if he took the anarchists for granted. They didn't know that Bookchin thought they were sinking swiftly into ideological and moral decay.

They do now. Bookchin views-with-alarm almost every new tendency in anarchism except his own specialty, ecology. What's more, the nefarious novelties exhibit malign thematic affinities. Not only are they pernicious, they are pernicious in essentially the same way. They represent a recrudescence of an old heresy, "individualism," decked out in trendy post-modernist fashions in a configuration Bookchin calls "lifestyle anarchism." Much worse than a falling-away from some aspects of classical left-wing anarchism, lifestyle anarchism is (he insists) fundamentally opposed to the defining tenets of anarchism. (How this could have happened on *his* watch he does not explain.)

For Bookchin, then, lifestyle anarchists are not just errant comrades, they are traitors. As such they are even worse than avowed opponents of anarchism. He mistreats them accordingly. His jeremiad is downright nasty. There aren't many epithets he doesn't work in somewhere or another, and never mind if they sometimes contradict each other (for instance, "individualism" and "fascism" applied to the same people). They don't have to be true to be effective. Bookchin started out as a Stalinist, and it sure shows in the abusive style and unscrupulous content of his polemic. He wants no dialogue with his self-appointed enemies, only their irreparable discredit.

I get the distinct impression that Bookchin, an elderly man said to be in ill health, is cashing in his chips as a prominent anarchist theorist and staking all his influence and reputation on demolishing all possible alternatives to his own creed, what he calls "social anarchism." A parting shot.

He missed the target. He had to miss the target, since there is none. There's no such thing as "lifestyle anarchism." There are only a lot of anarchists exploring a lot of ideas — a lot of different ideas — that Bookchin disapproves of. It follows that *this* book is not a defense of "lifestyle anarchism." There's no such unicorn, so I couldn't defend it even if I wanted to. The very phrase is Bookchin's invention, much as Stalin invented a nonsense category, the "bloc of Rights and Trotskyists," to collect all his political enemies for their more convenient disposal. At the time, Bookchin believed this, and everything else, the Party told him to believe. He hasn't changed much; or, if he did, he's changed back.

If I were only taking Bookchin to task for his incivility, I'd be a hypocrite, for I've penned plenty of blunt critiques of various anarchists and anti-authoritarians. A Dutch anarchist, Siebe Thissen, has described me — not as a criticism — as the severest critic of contemporary anarchism (1996: 60). Maybe I am, although criticism of anarchists takes up only a fraction of the content of my previous three books. But I've often been tough on anarchists I considered authoritarian, dishonest or stupid.

Often harsh but, I like to think, rarely unfair. Some people, especially those I've criticized, mistake my being articulate for my being rude, or mistake my noticing them for being obsessed with them. Be that as it may, for me to set myself up as the Miss Manners of anarchism would not be appropriate. I do think Murray Bookchin needs a lesson in manners, and I'm going to give him one, but incivility is the least of what's wrong with his dyspeptic diatribe. It's what he says, far more than how he says it, that I mean to have done with.

I am not, except incidentally, defending those whom Bookchin targets as "lifestyle anarchists." (For the record, I'm not one of his identified targets.) I am debunking the very category of lifestyle anarchism as a construct as meaningless as it is malicious. And I am coming down with crushing force on "an ugly, stupid style and substance of

13

doctrinal harangue" (Black 1992: 189), the worst survival of Bookchin's original Marxism. I've done it before and, frankly, I rather resent having to do it again. Bookchin has made the cardinal author's mistake of falling for his own jacket blurbs. Otherwise he could never write such a wretched screed and hope to get away with it. His previous contributions to anarchism, even if they were as epochal as he likes to think, are no excuse for this kind of gutter-gabble. His swan-song sounds nothing but sour notes. And sour grapes.

Which is why I think there's a place for *my* polemic. If even the great Bookchin can't get away with talking trash, maybe less eminent anarchists will be less tempted to talk trash. If even the quasi-academic Bookchin's quasi-scholarship doesn't hold up under even modest scrutiny, maybe some unduly impressionable anarchists will learn to question the authority of footnotes and jacket blurbs. Better scholars than Bookchin live in dread of somebody someday looking up their footnotes. I'll be getting around to several of *them,* too. But, worst things first.

Most people will take no interest in what Bookchin and I have to say about anarchism. These books aren't destined for the best-seller lists. Even some feel-good anarchists will dismiss the ruckus as "in-fighting." But on one point at least I think Bookchin would agree with me: in-fighting can be as important as out-fighting. Indeed it's impossible to tell them apart. The fighting has a lot to do with determining who is in and who is out. But anybody who thinks that anarchism is, or might be, important should consider this controversy important. I admit I'm almost as vain as Bookchin, but maybe I *am* the "lifestyle anarchist" to call him out for a showdown at high noon out at the Circle-A Ranch.

A throwback to *vulgar* Marxism in more than one sense, *Social Anarchism or Lifestyle Anarchism* may turn out to be the last tract of its kind, at least the last one with anarchist pretensions. Soon there will be nobody left in North America with the requisite Leninist background to practice this highly stylized genre of defamation. Debunking it may assist anarchists in letting go of the leftism they have outgrown, some of them without realizing it. Cleansed of its leftist residues, anarchy — anarchism minus Marxism — will be free to get better at being what it is.

Chapter 1: Murray Bookchin, Grumpy Old Man

Social Anarchism or Lifestyle Anarchism may well be the worst book about anarchists that any of them has ever written.

According to the cover blurb, Murray Bookchin, born in 1921, has been "a lifelong radical since the early 1930s." "Radical" is here a euphemism for "Stalinist"; Bookchin was originally "a militant in the Young Pioneers and the Young Communist League" (Clark 1990:102; cf. Bookchin 1977:3). Later he became a Trotskyist. At one time Bookchin himself, "as one who participated actively in the 'radical' movements of the thirties" (1970: 56), put the word "radical," considering the context, in quotation marks, but now he is nostalgic about that milieu, what he calls the Left That Was (66–86).

About 25 years ago, Murray Bookchin peered into the mirror and mistook it for a window of opportunity. In 1963 he wrote, under a pseudonym, *Our Synthetic Society* (Herber 1963), which anticipated (although it seems not to have influenced) the environmentalist movement. In 1970, by which time he was pushing 50 and calling himself an anarchist, Bookchin wrote "Listen, Marxist!" — a moderately effective anti-authoritarian polemic against such Marxist myths as the revolutionary vanguard organization and the proletariat as revolutionary subject (Bookchin 1971:171–222). In this and in other essays collected in *Post-Scarcity Anarchism* (1971), Bookchin disdained to conceal his delight with the disarray of his Marxist comrades-turned-competitors. He thought he saw his chance. Under his tutelage, anarchism would finally displace Marxism, and Bookchin would place the stamp of his specialty, "social ecology," on anarchism. Not only would he be betting on the winning horse, he would be the jockey. As one of his followers has written, "if your efforts at creating your own mass movement have been pathetic failures, find someone else's movement and try to lead *it*" (Clark 1984: 108).

Bob Black

Bookchin thereupon set out to conquer the anarchists for the eco-radicals (the Greens), the Greens for the anarchists, and all for one — the great one — Murray Bookchin himself. He would supply the "muscularity of thought" (Bookchin 1987b: 3) that they lacked. By now he's been "a prophetic voice in the ecology movement for more than thirty years," if he does say so himself (Institute for Social Ecology 1996: 13) (Bookchin co-founded the ISE). He cranked out several well-padded, largely repetitious books. *The Ecology of Freedom* (1982; rev. ed. 1991) is the one he apparently regards as his magnum opus. At any rate, one of his jacket blurbs (Bookchin 1987a) quotes a revolutionary anarchist weekly, the *Village Voice,* to that effect (cf. Clark [1984]: 215).

The material base for these superstructural effusions was Bookchin's providential appointment as a Dean at Goddard College near Burlington, Vermont, a cuddle-college for hippies and, more recently, punks, with wealthy parents (cf. Goddard College 1995). He also held an appointment at Ramapo College. Bookchin, who sneers at leftists who have embarked upon "alluring university careers" (67), is one of them.

Something went awry. Although Dean Bookchin was indeed widely read by North American anarchists — one of his acknowledged sycophants (Clark 1984: 11) calls him "the foremost contemporary anarchist theorist" (Clark 1990: 102; cf. Clark 1982: 59) — in fact, not many anarchists acknowledged him as *their* dean. They appreciated his ecological orientation, to be sure, but some drew their own, more far-reaching conclusions from it. The Dean came up against an unexpected obstacle. The master-plan called for anarchists to increase in numbers and to read his books, and those parts came off tolerably well. It was okay if they also read a few anarchist classics, Bakunin and Kropotkin for instance (8), vetted by the Dean, with the understanding that even the best of them afford "mere glimpses" of the forms of a free society (Bookchin 1971: 79) subsequently built upon, but transcended by, the Dean's own epochal discovery, social ecology/social anarchism. Bookchin does not mind standing on the shoulders of giants — he rather enjoys the feel of them under his heel — so long as he stands tallest of all.

He must have had no doubt that he would. He seemed to have no competition intramurally. Paul Goodman, "the most widely known anarchist" (De Leon 1978:132), untimely died. Tweedy British and Canadian anarchist intellectuals like Herbert Read, Alex Comfort and George Woodcock shuffled off into the literary world. Aging class-struggle fundamentalists like Sam Dolgoff and Albert Meltzer could be counted on to just keep doing what they were doing, whatever that was, and with their usual success. "We all stand on the shoulders of others," as the Dean generously allows (1982: Acknowledgements). Dean Bookchin could stand on the shoulders of midgets too. The footing was even surer there.

What the Dean did not expect was that anarchists would start reading outside his curriculum and, worse yet, occasionally *think for themselves*, something that — in all fairness — nobody could have anticipated. They read, for instance, about the ethnography of the only societies — certain of the so-called primitive societies — which have actually been operative anarchist societies on a long-term basis. They also read about plebeian movements, communities, and insurrections — Adamites, Ranters, Diggers, Luddites, Shaysites, Enrages, Carbonari, even pirates (to mention, to be brief, only Euro-American, and only a few Euro-American examples) — seemingly outside of the Marxist-Bookchinist progressive schema. They scoped out Dada and Surrealism. They read the Situationists and the pro-situs. And, yes, like earlier generations of anarchists, they were receptive to currents of cultural radicalism. Indeed, instead of listening to "decent music" (64 n. 37), they often preferred punk rock to Pete Seeger and Utah Philips ("the folk song," he has explained, "constitutes the emotional, aesthetic, and spiritual expression of a people" [Bookchin 1996: 19]). And usually their hair was either too long or too short. Who sent them down this twisted path?

In some cases it was the "self-styled anarchist" (1, 2,9) — this is a favorite Bookchin slur — who wrote:

The graffiti on the walls of Paris — "Power to the Imagination," "It is forbidden to forbid," "Life without dead times" [sic], "Never work" — represent a more probing analysis of these sources [of revolutionary unrest in modern society] than all the theoretical tomes inherited from the past. The uprising revealed that we are at the end of an old era and well into the beginning of a new one. The motive forces of revolution today, at least in the industrialized world, are not simply scarcity and material need, but also *the quality of everyday life,* the demand for the liberation of experience, the attempt to gain control over one's destiny [emphasis in the original].

This was not a solemn revolt, a *coup d'etat* bureaucratically plotted and manipulated by a "vanguard" party; it was witty, satirical, inventive and creative — and therein lay its strength, its capacity for immense self-mobilization, its infectiousness.

The lumpen-bohemian crazy who penned this paean to "neo-Situationist 'ecstasy'" (26) is the prelapsarian Murray Bookchin (1971: 249–250, 251), These are all, in fact, situationist slogans. Some of us believed him then. Now he tells us we were wrong, although he never tells us *he* ever was. Why should we believe him now?

The Hard Right Republicans like Newt Gingrich along with the Neo-Conservative intellectuals (most of the latter, like the Dean, being high-income, elderly Jewish ex-Marxists from New York City who ended up as journalists and/or academics) blame the decline of Western civilization on the '60s. Bookchin can't credibly do that, since it was in the '60s that he came out as an anarchist, and built up the beginnings of his reputation as a theorist. In his golden years, he has to tread very carefully on this dark and bloody ground:

For all its shortcomings, the anarchic counterculture during the early part of the hectic 1960s was often intensely political and cast expressions like desire and ecstasy in eminently social terms, often deriding the personalistic tendencies of the later Woodstock generation (9).

By definition "the early part of the hectic 1960s" is presumably the years 1960–1964. This is the first time I've heard tell of an "anarchic counterculture" during the Kennedy Administration. As manifested in — what? the Peace Corps? the Green Berets? And while there were personalistic tendencies in the early 1960s, no one then anticipated, and so no one derided, the specific "personalistic tendencies of the later Woodstock generation." Not Bookchin, certainly, who concluded prematurely that "Marxian predictions that Youth Culture would fade into a comfortable accommodation with the system have proven to be false" (1970: 60).

What did the all-seeing Dean do to combat these nefarious trends in the 20-odd years they have been infecting anarchism? Nothing. He had better things to do than come to the rescue of the anarchist ideology he considers the last best hope of humankind. On the one hand, he was consolidating his alluring academic career; on the other, he was making a play for ideological hegemony over the Green movement. Were we all supposed to wait up for him?

There were those who actually tried to implement the Dean's directive to formulate "a coherent program" and "a revolutionary organization to provide a direction for the mass discontent that contemporary society is creating" (1). Note that Bookchin demands *one* organization, although he does not say if he wants an American CNT, an American FAI, or an American symbiote of both such as formed in Spain, with less than entirely positive consequences (Bookchin 1994: 20–25; cf. Brademas 1953).

During the recent decades of decadence, there were several opportunities for the Dean to participate in this important work. He claims that his parents were Wobblies (2–3) — I wonder what they thought when he became a Communist? — but he did not himself join the Industrial Workers of the World although it still, after a fashion, exists. In the late 1970s, some class-struggle anarchists formed the Anarchist Communist Federation, which collapsed in acrimony after a few years. The Dean did not join. One ACF faction set up the syndicalist Workers Solidarity Alliance; Bookchin didn't join that one either. And finally, in the last few years the direct-actionist newspaper *Love & Rage* has tried to turn its support groups into the nuclei of a national anarchist organization. Once again, Bookchin held himself aloof.

Why? No doubt all these organizations fell somewhat short of his requirements, but as my mother says, "what do you want, an egg in your beer?" The CNT and the FAI were also imperfect. Everything is imperfect. If your fundamental critique of contemporary North American anarchists is that they have failed to assemble in a continental federation, surely you should have told them what is to be done, and how, a long time ago. The involvement of so distinguished a militant as Bookchin might energize an organization which might otherwise appear to be a sect of squabbling, droning dullards, perhaps because, in each and every instance, it *is* a sect of squabbling, droning dullards.

The only possible justification is that — to do justice to the Dean (and do I *ever* want to do exactly that!) — he laid down two requirements, not just one. A directive organization, yes — but with "a coherent program." Such time as remained after the performance of his administrative and academic responsibilities (and the lecture circuit) the Dean has devoted to providing the coherent program. No doubt Bookchin can organize the masses (he must have had a lot of practice, and surely great success, in his Marxist-Leninist days). So can many other comrades — but no other comrade can concoct a coherent program the way Bookchin can. It is, therefore, only rational for a division of labor to prevail. Less talented comrades should do the organizational drudge-work, freeing up Dean Bookchin — after hours — to theorize. It's an example of what capitalist economists call the Law of Comparative Advantage. All of that Kropotkinist-Bookchinist talk about rotation of tasks, about superseding the separation of hand-work and brain-work — time enough for that *after* the Revolution.

The Dean's booklet thunders (in a querulous sort of a way) that "anarchism stands at a turning point in its long and turbulent history" (1). When didn't it? In the time-honored sophist manner, the Dean offers an answer to a nonsense question of his own concoction. "At a time when popular distrust of the state has reached extraordinary proportions in many countries," etc., etc., "the failure of anarchists — or, at least, many self-styled anarchists — to reach a potentially huge body of supporters" is due, not entirely of course, but "in no small measure to the changes that have occurred in many anarchists over the past two decades... [they] have slowly surrendered the social core of anarchist ideas to the all-pervasive Yuppie and New Age personalism that marks this decadent, bourgeoisified era" (1).

Now this is a curious claim. Anarchism is unpopular, not because it opposes popular ideological fashions, but because it embraces them? It's unpopular because it's popular? This isn't the first time I've identified this obvious idiocy (Black & Gunderloy 1992).

Simple logic aside (where Dean Bookchin cast it), the Dean's empirical assumptions are ridiculous. North American anarchism is not "in retreat" (59), it has grown dramatically in the last twenty years. The Dean might have even had a little to do with that. It is *leftism* which is in retreat. That this growth of anarchism has coincided with the eclipse of orthodox anarcho-leftism by more interesting varieties of anarchy doesn't conclusively prove that the heterodox anarchies are the growth sector, but it sure looks that way. For instance, the North American anarchist publication with the highest circulation, *Anarchy: A Journal of Desire Armed,* is on Bookchin's enemies list (39, 50).

As for the supposition that "Yuppie and New Age personalism" are "all-pervasive" in our "decadent, bourgeoisified era," this says more about Dean Bookchin and the company he keeps than it does about contemporary society. If you are an upper middle class academic in an affluent leftist enclave like Burlington or Berkeley, you might well think so, but to generalize those impressions to the general society is unwarranted and narcissistic ("personalistic," as it were). America (or Canada) is still much more like Main Street than Marin County. If the Dean really thinks the brat-pack collegians in his Burlington ashram are representative North American youth, he doesn't get out enough.

Berating "Yuppies" for their self-indulgence, something Bookchin carries to the point of obsession (1 & *passim),* doesn't defy media-managed popular opinion, it *panders* to it. As is typical of progressives, Bookchin is behind the times. Not only are the '60s over, as he has finally figured out, so are the '70s and the '80s. The Old Left that he nostalgically recalls, what he calls the Left That Was (66–86), extolled discipline, sacrifice, hard work, monogamy, technological progress, heterosexuality, moralism, a sober and orderly if not downright puritanical lifestyle, and the subordination of the personal ("selfishness") to the interest of the cause and the group (be it the party, the union or the affinity group):

The puritanism and work ethic of the traditional left stem from one of the most powerful forces opposing revolution today — the capacity of the bourgeois environment to infiltrate the revolutionary framework. The origins of this power lie in the commodity nature of man under capitalism, a quality that is almost automatically translated to the organized group — and which the group, in turn, reinforces in its members.

This passage might have been written by Jacques Camatte, whose essay "On Organization" has exerted an anti-organizational influence on a lot of us "lifestyle anarchists" (Camatte 1995: 19–32). By now the reader will be on to my game (one of them, anyway): the above-quoted author is once again Bookchin the Younger (1971: 47; cf. Bookchin 1977: ch. 11). Again:

In its demands for tribalism, free sexuality, community, mutual aid, ecstatic experience, and a balanced ecology, the Youth Culture prefigures, however inchoately, a joyous communist and classless society, freed of the trammels of hierarchy and domination, a society that would transcend the historic splits between town and country, individual and society, and mind and body (Bookchin 1970: 59).

Bookchin the Elder's values, in contrast, are precisely those of the New Right and the neo-conservatives who have set the country's current political and ideological agendas — not the New Age bubbleheads Bookchin may meet in Vermont's socialist Congressman Bernie Saunders' hot tub.

"Yuppie" is, on the Dean's lips, an ill-chosen epithet. It is (lest we forget) a neologism and semi-acronym for "young urban professional." To which aspects of this conjuncture does Dean Bookchin object? To urbanism? Bookchin is the apostle of urbanism (1987): he thinks that "some kind of urban community is not only the environment of humanity: it is its destiny" (1974: 2). To professionalism? A college professor/bureaucrat such as Bookchin is a professional. The high technology Bookchin counts on to usher in post-scarcity anarchism (1971: 83–135; 1989: 196) is the invention of professionals and the fever-dream of techno-yuppies. So if Dean Bookchin, an *old* urban professional, disparages young urban professionals, what is it about them that he hates so much? By a process of elimination, it cannot be that they are urban and it cannot be that they are professional. It must be that they are *young,* as the Dean is not. Actually, a lot of them aren't all that young — most are baby boomers entering middle age — but to a Grumpy Old Man of 75 like Dean Bookchin, that's young enough to resent. But it's not their fault, after all, that most of them will live on long after Murray Bookchin is dead and forgotten.

And one more thing: Now that we know why the heretical anarchists have "failed to reach a potentially huge body of supporters," what's *his* excuse? One of his editors calls him "arguably the most prolific anarchist writer" (Ehrlich 1996: 384). (Although he has yet to outproduce the late Paul Goodman, who "produced a stream of books containing some of his enormous output of articles and speeches" (Walter 1972: 157) and he is likely to be soon surpassed by Hakim Bey — a far better writer — which may account for some of the insensate hatred the Dean displays for Bey.) So the truth is out there. Where, after all these years, are the Bookchinist masses?

The Dean's vocabulary of abuse evokes what he calls the Left That Was (66) but hardly the fondness he feels for it. His epithets for unorthodox anarchists are the standard Stalinist epithets for all anarchists. He berates anarchist "decadence" over and over, to which he often appends abstract denunciations of "bourgeois" or "petty bourgeois" tendencies. "Decadence" is an epithet so indiscriminately applied that a spirited case has been made for retiring it from responsible discourse (Gilman 1975). Even without going quite so far, undeniably "'decadent' as a term of political and social abuse has a generous range of applications," especially as deployed by Marxists and Fascists (Adams 1983: 1).

To speak of the Dean's denunciations of *le bourgeois* as "abstract" is my characteristically courteous way of hinting that he of all people had better pick his words more carefully. I say "abstract" because a college dean is a member of the bourgeoisie if, in any objective sense, anybody is. Bookchin surely has a higher income than anybody he's targeted. Dean Bookchin has to be deploying the word in a subjective, moralistic, judgmental sense which, however, he isn't defining.

It never used to bother the Dean that "many militant radicals tend to come from the relatively affluent strata" (Bookchin 1971: 25) — as his student disciples still do. Who else can afford to sit at his feet? For 1996–1997, the two-semester masters' program in Social Ecology costs $10,578 (Goddard College 1996). Back then he considered it a "historic breach" that it was "relatively affluent middle class white youth" who created the implicitly revolutionary Youth Culture (Bookchin 1970: 54–55).

No one can possibly pronounce with any confidence upon the class position of present-day North American anarchists in general, much less the class positions of "individualists," Bookchinists, etc. (Although my impression is that most anarcho-syndicalists are campus-based and none of them are factory workers. Work is much easier to glorify than it is to perform.) Nor does it bother the Dean that almost the only luminaries unconditionally admitted to his anarchist pantheon, Bakunin and Kropotkin, were hereditary aristocrats. Class-baiting is evidently a weapon to be deployed with fine discrimination.

For Bookchin, as for Stalinists, class is not a category of analysis, only an argot of abuse. Long ago he dismissed "workeritis" as *reactionary to the core"* rendered meaningless by the trans-class decomposition of contemporary society (1971: 186–187). So completely did class disappear from Bookchin's ideology that a review of one of his goofier books (Bookchin 1987) exclaimed that "it is what is missing altogether that renders his book terminally pathetic. Nowhere does he find fault with the most fundamental dimension of modern living, that of wage-labor and the commodity" (Zerzan 1994: 166). He now reverts to the hoary Marxist epithets — "bourgeois," "petit-bourgeois" and "lumpen" — but with no pretense that they have, for him, real social content. Otherwise, how could he apply all these words to the same people? In their relations to the means of production (or lack thereof), lifestyle anarchists cannot be both bourgeois and lumpens.

And how likely is it that out of these "thousands of self-styled anarchists" (1), not one is a proletarian?

Where Bookchin accuses rival anarchists of individualism and liberalism, Stalinists accuse all anarchists of the same. For example, there was that *Monthly Review* contributor who referred to Bookchinism as "a crude kind of individualistic anarchism" (Bookchin 1971: 225)! In other words,

...capitalism promotes egotism, not individuality or "individualism."...The term "bourgeois individualism," an epithet widely used today against libertarian elements, reflects the extent to which bourgeois ideology permeates the socialist project —

— these words being, of course, those of Bookchin the Younger (1971: 284). That the Dean reverts to these Stalinist slurs in his dotage reflects the extent to which bourgeois ideology permeates *his* project. Fanatically devoted to urbanism, the Dean was being complimentary, not critical, when he wrote that "the fulfillment of individuality and intellect was the historic privilege of the urban dweller or of individuals influenced by urban life" (1974: 1). Individuality's not so bad after all, provided it's on *his* terms.

As for "decadence," that is an eminently bourgeois swear-word for people perceived to be having more fun than you are. By now the word has lost whatever concrete meaning it ever had. Calling post-leftist anarchists "decadent" is just Dean Bookchin's way of venting his envy and, as Nietzsche would say, *ressentiment* that they are not afflicted with the hemorrhoids, tax audits, or whatever it is that's raining on *his* Mayday parade.

Chapter 2: What is Individualist Anarchism?

Dean Bookchin posits an eternally recurring "tension" within anarchism between the individual and the social (4). As this is none other than the central conundrum of Western political philosophy, the Dean is neither original nor — more important — has he identified a specifically anarchist tension. He goes on to identify the antitheses within anarchism as "two basically contradictory tendencies: a personalistic commitment to individual *autonomy* and a collectivist commitment to social *freedom*" (4). This is the "unbridgeable chasm" his book title refers to.

If the Dean is right — that individual autonomy and social liberation are not just in tension but *basically contradictory* — then anarchy *is* impossible, as anti-anarchists have always maintained. Bookchin here rejects out of hand what he used to espouse, "a society that would transcend the historic splits between...individual and society" (1970: 59).

Not all of us share his conservative fatalism. We too have our apprehensions and our times of despair. But to surrender to them entirely (which I condemn nobody for doing, if he's honest about it) is to renounce any affiliation with anarchism. The Dean won't fish, neither will he cut bait. He won't shit, neither will he get off the pot.

Some of those with impeccable, Bookchin-approved credentials, such as Kropotkin, had a more tolerant take on this genuinely tragic dilemma:

Anarchist Communism maintains that most valuable of all conquests — individual liberty — and moreover extends it and gives it a solid basis — economic liberty — without which political liberty is delusive; it does not ask the individual who has rejected god, the universal tyrant, god the king, and god the parliament, to give unto himself a god more terrible than any of the preceding — god the Community, or to abdicate upon its altar his independence, his will, his tastes, and to renew the vow of asceticism which he formerly made before the crucified god. It says to him, on the contrary, "No society is free so long as the individual is not so!" (Kropotkin 1890: 14–15)

Bookchin is the veritable high priest of what Kropotkin calls "god the Community," "more terrible than any of the preceding," the most vicious and oppressive god of all.

"Social freedom" is like the "free market" in the sense that the freedom referred to has to be metaphorical. It makes no literal sense to attribute freedom to behavioral interaction systems, even feedback systems, lacking the necessarily individual qualities of consciousness and intention. It's like saying an anthill or the solar system or a thermostat is free. Free from, and for, what? What else could a society or a market possibly be free *of* if not autonomous individuals?

If one assigns *any* value to individual autonomy, logically there are only two possibilities for it to even exist, much less flourish, in society. (Contrary to what the Dean implies [58], not even Max Stirner thought it was possible outside of society [1995: 161, 271–277].) The first is a compromise: liberalism. The individual exchanges part of his precarious natural liberty for society's protection of the rest of it, and also for the practical opportunities for advancing his interests only opened up in a social state. This was the position of Thomas Hobbes, John Locke, Adam Smith and William Blackstone. In the public sphere, freedom means democracy; In the private sphere, it means individual rights.

The second resolution of the quandary, the radical one, is anarchism. Anarchism rejects the dichotomy as false — maybe not false as existing society is constituted, but false in its supposed fatality. In an anarchist society the individual gains freedom, not at the expense of others, but in cooperation with them. A person who believes that this condition — anarchy — is possible and desirable is called an anarchist. A person who thinks it is not possible or not desirable is a statist.

As I shall have no difficulty demonstrating later on, it so happens that the Dean himself is not an anarchist, merely, in his own terminology, a "self-styled anarchist." But that's no reason for those of us who (albeit unenthusiastically, if I may speak for myself) *are* anarchists not to heed his critique. From George Bernard Shaw to Guy Debord, anti-anarchists who took anarchism seriously have often supplied crucial critiques the anarchists were unable or unwilling to construct themselves. Unfortunately, Bookchin's isn't one of them.

Bob Black

What is remarkable about Dean Bookchin's posturing as the Defender of the Faith, aside from the fact that he doesn't share it, is how many of the Church Fathers (and Mothers) he has excommunicated as "individualists." Predictably, William Godwin (5), Max Stirner (7, 11) and Benjamin Tucker (8) Bookchin summarily dismisses as individualists, although that hardly does justice to the richness of their insights and their relevance to *any* anarchism. (Although even Kropotkin acknowledged that Godwin espoused communism in the first edition of *Political Justice,* only "mitigating" that view in later editions [Kropotkin 1995; 238], and the anarcho-syndicalist Rudolf Rocker acknowledged that Godwin "was really the founder of the later communist Anarchism" [1947: 7].) 1

But that's only the beginning of the purge. The Dean condemns even Proudhon as an individualist (5), although he elsewhere pays tribute to "Proudhon's emphasis on federal-ism [which] still enjoys considerable validity" (Bookchin) 1996: 24). When Bookchin says that something from a classical anarchist still enjoys considerable validity, this is his way of saying that's whom he filched it from. The federalism of Proudhon's later years (1979) is virtually identical to Bookchin's call for a "confederation of decentralized municipalities" (60). Which is tantamount to saying that in the end Proudhon was not an anarchist, as I am not the only one to have noticed (Steven 1984). Indeed, the Dean has come close to admitting it himself (Bookchin 1977: 21).

The Dean now claims that the prominent Spanish anarchist Federica Montseney was a "Stirnerite" [*sic*] in theory if not in practice (8). In his *The Spanish Anarchists* she is "one of the FAI's luminaries" (Bookchin 1977: 243). The FAI was a "vanguard" (the word is Bookchin's) anarcho-communist secret society (Bookchin 1994: 21–22; cf. Brademas 1953).

Even Emma Goldman is under a cloud. Although she was an avowed anarcho-communist, she also displayed a disqualifying affinity with Nietzsche (8), and she was, after all, "by no means the ablest thinker in the libertarian pantheon" (13). Bookchin has a muscular, masculine disdain for anarchist women such as Emma Goldman, Federica

Montseney and L. Susan Brown. Only his innate modesty kept the
Dean from naming who *is* the ablest thinker in the libertarian
pantheon, but then again, who, having read him, needs to be told?

Paul Goodman, a "communitarian anarchist" (Stafford 1972: 112),
Bookchin calls "an essentially individualistic anarchist" (12), although
Goodman was *essentially* an urban-oriented, humanistic anarcho-
collectivist (Goodman & Goodman 1961: ch. 6 & 220; cf. Stafford
1972: 112–113) from whom Bookchin has cribbed many ideas
without admitting it. Notice, for instance, the remarkable absence of
any inferences to the by then deceased Goodman in Bookchin's *The
Limits of the City* (1974) or *The Rise of Urbanization and the Decline
of Citizenship* (1987), although he did let slip the name in *Crisis in
Our Cities* (Herber 1965: 177) at a time when Goodman was in his
prime whereas the future Dean was so far from foreseeing his own
celebrity that he wrote under a pseudonym. He'll soon wish he'd
written *this* trashy had under a pseudonym.

"Individualist" anarchists in the original sense — people like Max
Stirner (1995) and John Henry Mackay — were never numerous, as
Bookchin observes with too much satisfaction (6–8). And they were
always few and far between, strange to say, in decadent, bourgeois
North America, supposedly their natural breeding-ground. Stirner did
not identify himself as an anarchist, probably because the only
(indeed, the very first) "self-styled" anarchist in the 1840s when he
was writing was Proudhon, for whom moralism, as Stirner noticed,
served as a surrogate for religion (*ibid.*: 46) — as it does for the Dean.
The rather few individuals who at later times considered themselves
Stirnerists have, however, usually considered themselves anarchists as
well, such as the Italian peasant guerrilla Renzo Novatore (Black &
Parfrey 1989: 92–93)

It is worth mentioning — because so many people who toss his name
around have never read him — that Stirner had no social or economic
program whatsoever. He was no more pro-capitalist than he was pro-
communist, although Marxists like Marx, Engels and Bookchin have
routinely and mindlessly castigated him as an apologist for capitalism.
Stirner was just not operating at that level. He was staking a claim, the

most radical claim possible, for the individual as against all the ideologies and abstractions which, purporting to liberates him in general and in the abstract, left the individual as personally, practically subordinate as ever: "In principle... Stirner created a *utopistic vision of individuality* that marked a new point of departure for the affirmation of personality in an increasingly impersonal world" (Bookchin 1982: 159). From Stirner's perspective — which on this point is also mine — ideologies like liberalism, humanism, Marxism, syndicalism, and Bookchinism have all too much in common (cf. Black 1994: 221–222).

Nobody the Dean denounces as a "Stirnerite," not Michael William (50), not Hakim Bey (23) is a Stirnerist if this implies that he affirms amoral egoism *and* is indifferent to or entirely agnostic about social and economic formations. Both obviously assume as axiomatic the need for a social matrix for individual efflorescence. What distinguishes them, in more than one sense, from the Dean is their appreciation of the epistemic break in bourgeois thought wrought by the likes of Stirner and Nietzsche:

A sense of incompleteness haunts Western philosophy after Hegel's death and explains much of the work of Kierkegaard, Schopenhauer, Stirner, Nietzsche, the surrealists and the contemporary existentialists. For the Marxians merely to dismiss this post-Hegelian development as "bourgeois ideology" is to dismiss the problem itself.

You guessed it: Bookchin the Younger again (1971: 276). For Bookchin to dismiss this post-Hegelian development as "bourgeois ideology" is to dismiss the problem itself.

In a more recent, still narrower sense, "individualism" designates those who combine rejection of government with espousal of an absolutely unlimited laissez-faire market system. Such ideologues do exist, but Bookchin never even mentions a contemporary example, although he cannot be unaware of their existence, since he made use of one of their publishers, Free Life Books (Bookchin 1977). Considerable contact with some of them over the years has persuaded me that most anarcho-capitalists are sincere in their anarchism, although I am as certain that anarcho-capitalism is self-contradictory as I am that anarcho-syndicalism is. Unlike the Dean, I've on occasion taken the trouble to confute these libertarians (Black 1986:141–148; Black 1992: 43–62). But the point is, *nobody* the Dean targets in this screed is by any stretch of the imagination (not that he has one) an "individualist" anarchist in the usual contemporary sense of the term. He never even *claims* that any of them are.

The Dean makes the bizarre allegation that those he calls lifestyle anarchists, decadent successors to the individualist anarchists, claim (the quotation marks are his) their "sovereign rights" (12):

Their ideological pedigree is basically liberal, grounded in the myth of the fully autonomous individual whose claims to self-sovereignty are validated by axiomatic "natural rights," "intrinsic worth," or, on a more sophisticated level, an intuited Kantian transcendental ego that is generative of all knowable reality (11).

A digression on the, for lack of a better word, ethics of punctuation marks is in order here. "Quotation marks," wrote Theodor Adorno,

...are to be rejected as an ironic device. For they exempt the writer from the spirit whose claim is inherent in irony, and they violate the very concept of irony by separating it from the matter at hand and presenting a predetermined judgment on the subject. The abundant ironic quotation marks in Marx and Engels are the shadows that totalitarian methods cast in advance upon their writings, whose intention was the opposite: the seed from which eventually came what Karl Kraus called *Moskauderwelsch* [Moscow double-talk, from *Moskau*, Moscow, and *Kauderwelsch*, gibberish or double-talk]. The indifference to linguistic expression shown in the mechanical delegation of intention to a typographic cliché arouses the suspicion that the very dialectic that constitutes the theory's content has been brought to a standstill and the object assimilated to it from above, without negotiation. Where there is something which needs to be said, indifference to literary form almost always indicates dogmatization of the content. The blind verdict of quotation marks is its graphic gesture (Adorno 1990: 303).

Bob Black

As a tenured academic, the Dean is presumably aware that in scholarly discourse — and surely his magisterial essay is such — quotation marks identify *quotations*, yet his 45 footnotes fail to reference any use of these expressions by anybody. That is because no such quotations exist. So-called lifestyle anarchists (meaning: non-Bookchinists) don't usually think or write that way. They tend not to go in for rights-talk because it is just an ideological, mystifying way of saying what they want, something better said honestly and directly.

By this maladroit misrepresentation, the Dean inadvertently exposes his original misunderstanding of the so-called individualist anarchists. Max Stirner was an amoral egoist or individualist. Godwin and Proudhon were, if they were individualists at all, moralistic individualists preoccupied with what they called justice. Lysander Spooner was an example of a clearly moralistic, natural-rights individualist anarchist. But when the prominent individualist publisher Benjamin Tucker went over to Stirnerist egoism in the late nineteenth century, he split the American individualists. (This, as much as the competition from collectivists credited by Bookchin [6- 7], brought about the decline of the tendency.) Although there were exceptions, the moralistic natural-rights individualists — which were most of them — usually ended up as essentially advocates of pure free-market capitalism. Those attracted to the amoralist, egoist or (if you please) "Stirnerist" position necessarily shared with Stirner a whole-sale rejection of moralism, that being what Stirner, and Nietzsche after him, absolutely exploded as a tenable point of view. But no more than Stirner did they exhibit any interest in laissez-faire (or any) economics. Capitalism, as Max Weber noticed, has its own moralism, often if not always expressed as the "Protestant ethic." The egoists/amoralists and the free-market natural-rightists parted over precisely this point. The egoist/amoralists *have* contributed something to the "lifestyle anarchists," the natural-rightists have not.

For instance, take L. Susan Brown (please! — no, just kidding), who's attempted, says the Dean, "to articulate and elaborate a basically individualist anarchism, yet retain some filiations with anarcho-communism" (13), In a footnote he's more candid: "Brown's hazy commitment to anarcho-communism seems to derive more from her own preference than from her analysis" (62). In other words, maybe she means well but she's just a ditzy dame, like Emma Goldman. Just *believing* in anarcho-communism isn't good enough to acquit you of the charge of individualism. You have to emote a politically correct, anti-individualist "analysis" too. I wonder how many Makhnovists, and how many Spanish rank-and-file insurrectionaries fighting for *comunismo libertario* would have passed whatever final exam our pedant might assign to them to test their "analysis." I have a pretty good idea how they would have received such an insolent inquisition. Post-situationist that I am, I am far from sure that "the revolution will not be televised," but I am quite sure it will not be on the final exam, not if teacher knows what's good for him. As Marx so truly said, the educator himself needs educating. And as Diogenes said, why not whip the teacher when the student misbehaves?

The Dean has brought "down to date" (as Mark Twain would say) the New England Puritan exercise known as the "relation of faith." In order to join the Congregational Church, the applicant not only had to affirm each and every tenet of Calvinism, he had to demonstrate that he had gone through a standardized sequence of spiritual experiences. (Alcoholics Anonymous is the only Protestant cult which still imposes this requirement.) Most believers never made it that far. What the Dean means by an inadequate "analysis" is obvious enough: any analysis other than Bookchinism is no analysis at all. The "disdain for theory" he ascribes to "individualist" anarchism (11) is really disdain for, or rather indifference to, *his* theory. Nowadays, anarcho-communism is Bookchinism or it is nothing — according to Bookchin (60).

Like it or not — personally (and "personalistically"), I like it — there's an irreducible individualistic dimension to anarchism, even social anarchism, as L. Susan Brown is hardly heretical in pointing out (1993: ch. 1). According to Kropotkin, Anarcho-Communism says that "No society is free so long as the individual is not!" (1890: 15). If it sounds as if anarchism has, as the Dean might say, "filiations" with liberalism, that's because anarchism *does* have filiations with liberalism. What else could the Dean possibly mean when he writes that social anarchism is "made of fundamentally different stuff" than lifestyle anarchism, it is "heir to the Enlightenment tradition" (56)? As anarcho-syndicalist Rudolf Rocker wrote (and he was only summarizing the obvious):

In modern Anarchism we have the confluence of the two great currents which during and since the French Revolution have found such characteristic expression in the intellectual life of Europe: Socialism and Liberalism....

Anarchism has in common with Liberalism the idea that the happiness and the prosperity of the individual must be the standard in all social matters. And, in common with the great representatives of Liberal thought, it has also the idea of limiting the functions of government to a minimum. Its supporters have followed this thought to its ultimate logical consequences, and wish to eliminate every institution of political power from the life of society (1947: 16, 18–19).

If he hadn't seen these words before, the Dean would have come across part of these passages as quoted by Brown (1993:110). Naturally he'd rather debunk Brown, an obscure young academic (Jarach 1996), than the illustrious anarchist elder Rocker. Bookchin's a playground bully who doesn't mind hitting a girl with glasses, but he'd be off his Rocker to mess with Rudolf.

Nobody chooses his ancestors. Rationally, no one should be ashamed of them. Visiting the sins of the fathers on the children, even unto the fourth generation (Exodus 34:7) — as the Dean is doing, pretty much on schedule — hardly comports with the Enlightenment rationalism he claims as *his* ancestry (21, 56).

The Left That Was which provided Bookchin's original politics, Marxism-Leninism, also supplied him with a muscular polemical praxis and a versatile vocabulary of abuse. I've already drawn attention to one of these gambits, denigration-by-quotation-marks. Its "filiations" include Lenin's *"Left-Wing" Communism, an Infantile Disorder* (1940) and countless texts by Marx and Engels, as Adorno (1990) noticed. John Zerzan, reviewing Bookchin (1987), noted a related way that the Dean abused quotation marks: "Another device is to ignore the real history of urban life, as if illusory; he resorts at times to putting such terms as 'elected' representatives, 'voters' and 'taxpayers' in quotes as though the terms really don't, somehow, correspond to reality" (Zerzan 1994: 165). As if to confirm that he's incorrigible, Bookchin refers to this review, not as a review, but as a "review" (59). Bookchin was doing the same thing almost 40 years ago when the first chapter of *The Limits of the City* (1974: ix) was written: Tenochtitlan was the "capital," not the capital, of the urban, imperialistic, cannibalistic Aztec empire (*ibid.*: 7, 9).

Bookchin just doesn't know when to shut up. Having lambasted individualists as liberals, he turns around and insinuates that they are fascists! Critics of industrial technology (specifically, George Bradford of the *Fifth Estate*) who argue that it determines, as well as being determined by, social organization are, opines the Dean, "deeply rooted in the conservative German romanticism of the nineteenth century" which "fed into National Socialist ideology, however much the Nazis honored their antitechnological ideology in the breach" (29). This would be a sophisticated version of guilt-by-association if it were sophisticated. The Dean doesn't bother to even identify these "conservative German" romantics — he hasn't read them, probably couldn't even name them — much less substantiate their unlikely influence on contemporary "lifestyle" anarchists. Retro-leftist that he is, Bookchin must suppose that bracketing the hate-words "conservative" and "German" is a one-two punch nobody recovers from. One page later (30), he admits that "there is no evidence that Bradford is familiar with Heidegger or Jünger," the twentieth-century German intellectuals he *j'accuses* as carriers of nineteenth-century conservative German romantic ideology.

McCarthyism is the political strategy of guilt by association. If you know a Communist, or if you know someone who knows someone who is a Communist, presumptively *you* are a Communist and you'll have to talk your way out of it, preferably by ratting somebody out. The ex-Communist Bookchin has outdone Senator McCarthy. The Senator sought to uncover association as evidence of guilt. The Dean affirms guilt as evidence of association. That's really all there is to his dirty little diatribe. To be even *less* fair than Joe McCarthy is quite an accomplishment, what Nietzsche used to call a "downgoing."

Bob Black

And another thing, nineteenth-century romanticism was neither exclusively conservative nor exclusively German. What about the liberal or radical German romanticism of Beethoven and Büchner and Schiller and Heine? And what about the non-German radical romanticism of Blake and Burns and Byron and Shelley?

The Dean relates that the Nazis honored their romantic, anti-technological ideology "in the breach." "Honored in the breach" is Bookchin's poor try at heading off the obvious, and decisive, objection that the Nazis didn't *have* an anti-technological ideology. The *Autobahn* was as much a monument to technology as were its contemporaries the Moscow subway and the New York World's Fair (which, I suspect, thrilled the 18 year old Murray Bookchin). So was the V-2. Almost openly erotic references to iron and steel recur with monotonous and pathological frequency in Nazi rhetoric. As John Zerzan remarked in a book the Dean claims to have read (39–42, 62 n. 19);

Behind the rhetoric of National Socialism, unfortunately, was only an acceleration of technique, even into the sphere of genocide as a problem of industrial production. For the Nazis and the gullible, it was, again a question of how technology is understood ideally, not as it really is. In 1940 the General Inspector for the German Road System put it this way: "Concrete and stone are material things. Man gives them form and spirit. National Socialist technology possesses in all material achievement ideal content" (Zerzan 1994: 140).

I'm not one of those who cries out in horror at the slightest whiff of anti-Semitism. But the Dean sees fit to insinuate that even the promiscuously pluralistic Hakim Bey is ideologically akin to Hitler (22), and that the primitivist quest to recover authenticity "has its roots in reactionary romanticism, most recently in the philosophy of Martin Heidegger, whose *völkisch* 'spiritualism,' latent in *Being and Time,* later emerged in his explicitly fascist works" (50). So let's consider whether Bookchin-vetted classical anarchists are ideologically kosher. Proudhon was notoriously anti- Semitic (Silbener 1948), but since Bookchin dismisses him, however implausibly, as too much the individualist (4–5), let's set Proudhon aside. Bakunin, the Russian aristocrat who "emphatically prioritized the social over the individual" (5) had a notion what was wrong with his authoritarian rival, Karl Marx. Bakunin considered Marx, "the German scholar, in his threefold capacity as an Hegelian, a Jew, and a German," to be a "hopeless statist" (1995:142). A Hegelian, a Jew, a sort-of scholar, a Marxist, a hopeless (city-) statist — does this sound like anybody familiar?

The Dean approvingly quotes Lewis Mumford on "the esthetic excellence of the machine form" (32), a phrase which might have been turned by Marinetti or Mussolini or anyone else on the ill-defined frontier between Futurism and Fascism (cf. Moore 1996: 18). In *War, the Worlds Only Hygiene*, Marinetti elaborated on the Bookchin/Mumford aesthetic:

We are developing and proclaiming a great new idea that runs through modern life: the idea of mechanical beauty. We therefore exalt love for the machine, the love we notice flaming on the cheeks of mechanics scorched and smeared with coal. Have you never seen a mechanic lovingly at work on the great powerful body of his locomotive? His is the minute, loving tenderness of a lover caressing his adored woman (Flint 1972: 90).

The Germans conquered Europe with Panzers and Stukas not by blood-and-soil hocus-pocus. Nazi ideology is far tool incoherent to be characterized as either pro- or anti-technological. The Dean in bewailing our "decadent, bourgeoisified era" (1) and our "decadent personalism" (2) is himself echoing Nazi and Stalinist rhetoric, as he surely remembers, and it's as empty as ever. The point is that the ideology didn't have to make sense to matter. It was vague and inconsistent so as to appeal to as many people as possible who desperately needed something to believe in, something to free them from freedom, something to command their loyalty. It didn't have to be the same come-on for everyone. The Nazis, fishers of *Menschen,* understood that you need different bait to hook different fish, that's all.

And finally, individualist anarchists are *terrorists* — or rather, anarchist terrorists are individualists.

37

Bob Black

The inseparable association of anarchism with terrorism commenced for Americans with a specific event: the Haymarket tragedy in Chicago in 1886. As the police were breaking up a peaceable workers' rally, someone threw a bomb into their midst, killing or wounding several of them. Eight prominent anarchists involved in the union movement, but indisputably innocent of the bombing, were convicted of murder and four of them hanged (one committed suicide) on the basis of their anarchist agitation and beliefs. If there is one fact about the history of anarchism known to everyone who knows at least one fact about the history of anarchism, it is this: "Thereafter, anarchism, in the public mind, was inseparably linked with terrorism and destruction" (Avrich 1984: 428; cf. Schuster 1932: 166; Woodcock 1962: 464). And the anarchism with which the link was forged was the collectivist anarchism of the Haymarket defendants. That they were, as individuals, innocent is irrelevant to the genesis of the mad-bomber legend. Innocent in act but not necessarily in intention: "One of them, [Louis] Lingg, had the best alibi: he wasn't there... he was home, making bombs. He was thus convicted of a crime he would have *liked* to commit" (Black & Parfrey 1989: 67). In contrast, one historian refers to "the peaceful philosophy of Individualist Anarchism" (Schuster 1932: 159).

The anarchists' terrorist reputation was not, however, entirely fabricated by their enemies (Black 1994: 50–55). In the 1880s, left-wing European anarchists had already begun to preach, and practice, "propaganda by the deed," such as bombings — "chemistry," as they sometimes put it — and assassinations. Even the beatific Kropotkin was originally a supporter of "the new tactic" (Bookchin 1977: 115). Some thought it the most effective way to dramatize anarchism and disseminate it to the masses. According to what the Dean calls "the best account of Spanish Anarchism from 1931 to 1936" (Bookchin 1977: 325), "the last decade of the [nineteenth] century was one in which the anarchists really were engaged in the bomb-throwing which is popularly thought to exhaust their range of activities" (Brademas 1953: 9).

These anarchist terrorists were, to apply Bookchin's terminology anachronistically, usually social anarchists, rarely individualist anarchists. August Vaillant, who bombed the French Chamber of Deputies, was a leftist (Tuchman 1966: 91) and a member of an anarchist group (Bookchin 1977: 114). Of the French bombers of the 1890s, Ravachol alone, so far as anybody knows, was "almost but not quite" a Stirnerist (Tuchman 1964: 79).

The Spanish anarchists whom the Dean esteems above all others (1977, 1994) had perhaps the longest terrorist tradition of all. The index reference to "Terrorism, anarchist" in his history of Spanish anarchism covers dozens of pages (1977: 342). There were sporadic bombings in the 1880s which became chronic, at least in the anarchist stronghold of Barcelona, in the 1890s (Bookchin 1977: ch. 6). 1918–1923, period of violent class struggle in Spain, was the time of the *pistoleros* — gunmen — a term which applies to both employer-hired goons and anarcho-leftist militants. Among hundreds of others, "a premier, two former civil governors, an Arch-bishop, nearly 300 employers, factory directors, foremen, and police, and many workers and their leaders in the *sindicato libre* [a company union], fell before the bullets and bombs of Anarchist action groups" (Bookchin 1977: 191).

The *pistolero* phase subsided as the anarchists, who were getting the worst of the violence anyway, were driven underground by the Primo de Rivera dictatorship at the same time that a measure of prosperity took the edge off the class struggle. But anarcho-terrorism never ceased. During the '20s and '30s, "the FAI's most well-known militants — Durruti, the Ascaso brothers, Garcia Oliver — included terrorism in their repertory of direct action: 'Gunplay, especially in "expropriations" and in dealing with recalcitrant employers, police agents, and blacklegs, was not frowned upon'" (Bookchin 1994: 23). Their heists "sustained Ferrer-type schools, Anarchist printing presses, and a large publishing enterprise in Paris which produced the *Anarchist Encyclopedia,* as well as many books, pamphlets, and periodicals" (Bookchin 1977: 199).

I adduce these facts — and reference most of them, deliberately, to Bookchin — not to condemn or condone what "social anarchists" have sometimes done but to show up the Dean's duplicity. Terrorism has been, for better or for worse, a recurrent anarchist tactic for more than a century. And the anarcho-terrorists have almost always been "social," not individualist, anarchists. I've had occasion to rebut leftist falsifications to the contrary (Black 1994: 50–55). Bookchin justifies Spanish anarcho-*pistolero* terrorism as legitimate self-defense (1977: 201–202), an opinion I share, but the fact remains that it *was* terrorism — in Bookchinese, "social anarchist" terrorism — not the activity of individualist anarchists.

Chapter 3: Lifestyle Anarchism

As fast-and-loose as the Dean plays with the word "individualism," extrapolating it to something he calls "lifestyle anarchism" is, to borrow a phrase from Jeremy Bentham not just nonsense, it is nonsense on stilts. Here is how he does the stretch:

In the traditionally individualist-liberal United States and Britain, the 1990s are awash in self-styled [that word again!] anarchists who — their flamboyant radical rhetoric aside — are cultivating a latter-day anarcho-individualism that I will call *lifestyle anarchism*.... Ad hoc adventurism, personal bravura, an aversion to theory oddly akin to the antirational biases of postmodernism, celebrations of theoretical incoherence (pluralism), a basically apolitical and anti-organizational commitment to imagination, desire, and ecstasy, and an intensely self-oriented enchantment of [*sic*] everyday life, reflect the toll that social reaction has taken on Euro-American anarchism over the past two decades (9).

In a classic tale of cerebral fantasy, Jorge Luis Borges related that in Tlön, "the dominant notion is that everything is the work of one single author": "Criticism is prone to invent authors. A critic will choose two dissimilar works — the *Tao Te Ching* and the *1001 Nights*, let us say — and attribute them to the same writer, and then with all probity explore the psychology of this interesting *homme de lettres*...." (Monegal & Reid 1981: 118).

That is exactly the Dean's *modus operandi,* except that Borges was joking in a very sophisticated way whereas Bookchin is serious in a very dumb, dull way. Those he has designated "lifestyle anarchists" are essentially alike because, well, he has designated them as lifestyle anarchists. The label is self-verifying. He's cobbled together all his self-selected enemies who are also "self-styled" anarchists as "lifestyle anarchists." In an essay only recently published, but written In 1980, the Dean cogently observed that

...anarchism [has] acquired some bad habits of its own, notably an ahistorical and entrenched commitment to its own past. The decline of the New Left and the transformation of the sixties counter-culture into more institutionalized cultural forms compatible with the status quo created among many committed anarchists a longing for the ideological security and pedigree that also afflicts the dwindling Marxist sects of our day (1996: 23).

In the Middle Ages, what the Dean's doing — but they did it better back then, and in good faith — was known as Realism. There cannot be a name (goes the argument) unless there is something real which that name designates. St. Anselm's ontological argument for the existence of God, for instance, by defining God as that which nothing could be greater than, implies that God is the greatest possible being, and since *something* must be the greatest possible being, God must exist. The reflective reader will probably spot at least some of the flaws in this line of argument which almost all philosophers have long since recognized.

I am amazed to learn that the present epoch is "awash in self-styled anarchists." Maybe I should awash more often. I hadn't thought any place has been awash in self-styled anarchists since certain parts of Spain were in the 1930s. Maybe Burlington is awash in Bookchinists — a veritable Yankee Barcelona — but this conjecture is as yet unconfirmed.

"Lifestyle" wasn't always a dirty word for the Dean. Recalling what was wrong with the Stalinist '30s, he's written:

"Life-style?" — the word was simply unknown. If we were asked by some crazy anarchists how we could hope to change society without changing ourselves, our relations to each other, and our organizational structure, we had one ritualistic answer: "After the revolution...." (Bookchin 1970: 57).

Back then the Dean was calling for "communist life-styles" as integral to the revolutionary project (*ibid.*: 54). Today, the Dean alleges that lifestyle anarchism is "concerned with a 'style' rather than a society" (34), but the "crazy anarchists" he formerly identified with, but now maligns, agree with Bookchin the Younger that social revolution *is* lifestyle revolution, the revolution of everyday life: "It is plain that the goal of revolution today must be the liberation of daily life" (Bookchin 1971: 44).

Most of this gibberish is pejorative and content-free. If the dizzy Dean is saying anything substantive, he is claiming that those he has lumped (lumpened?) together as lifestyle anarchists are (1) anti-theoretical, (2) apolitical, (3) hedonistic and (4) anti-organizational. The question of organization is so large as to require a chapter in itself (Chapter 5). I'll take up the other charges here.

1.

Anti-Theoretical. As to this the Dean is nothing less than grotesque. When is a theorist not a theorist? When his theory is not the theory of Dean Bookchin. That disqualifies Guy Debord, Michel Foucault, Jacques Camatte, Jean Baudrillard and, to all intents and purposes, everybody published by Autonomedia. Bookchinism is not just the only true theory, it is the *only* theory. (Marxism, of course, is not theory, it is bourgeois ideology [Bookchin 1979].) Like Hegel and Marx before him, Bookchin likes to think that he is not only the finest but the *final* theorist. As they were wrong, so is he.

1.

Apolitical. This is, if anything, even zanier. How can a political philosophy like anarchism — any variety of anarchism — be apolitical? There is, to be sure, a difference between Bookchinism and all anarchisms. Anarchism is *anti-political* by definition. Bookchinism is political (specifically, it is city-statist, as shall shortly be shown). It follows as a matter of course that Bookchinism is incompatible with anarchism, but it doesn't follow that lifestyle anarchism is apolitical, only that lifestyle anarchism is, at worst, anarchism, and at best, contrary to Bookchinism.

1.

Hedonistic. Sure, why not?

The Dean is right about one thing: it's the truth (if no longer the whole truth) that anarchism continues the Enlightenment tradition. As such, it stands for life, liberty and the pursuit of happiness in a much more radical way than liberalism ever did. Godwin, for instance, argued that anarchism was the logical implication of utilitarianism. Kropotkin was convinced that "'the greatest happiness of the greatest number' is no longer a dream, a mere Utopia. *It is possible*" (1924: 4). His adoption of the utilitarian maxim was neither ironic nor critical.

Hedonism in some sense of the word has always been common ground for almost all anarchists. Rudolph Rocker attributed anarchist ideas to the Hedonists and Cynics of antiquity (1947: 5). Back before he lost his groove, the Dean praised the utopian socialist Charles Fourier for "envision[ing] new communities that would remove restrictions on hedonistic behavior and, almost embarrassingly to his disciples, sought to harmonize social relations on the basis of pleasure" (1974: 112). As that "most unsavory" (20) of lifestyle anarchists, Hakim Bey, put it, "your inviolable freedom awaits to be completed only by the love of other monarchs" (22 [quoting Bey 1991: 4]) — "words that could be inscribed on the New York Stock Exchange," grumps the Dean, "as a credo for egotism and social indifference" (22). Decadent degenerates that we are, lifestyle anarchists tend to favor "a state of things in which each individual will be able to give free rein to his inclinations, and even to his passions, without any other restraint than the love and respect of those who surround him." Presumably this credo, a more overtly hedonistic version of Bey's socially indifferent egotism, is even better suited to decorate the Stock Exchange — which would probably surprise its

Bob Black

author, the anarcho-communist Kropotkin (1890:15). We think *love* and *respect* could be forces as powerful as they are wonderful. Even Bakunin on occasion sounded more like Raoul Vaneigem than Jean-Jacques Rousseau, as when he wrote that the anarchist is distinguished by *"his frank and human selfishness,* living candidly and unsententiously for himself, and knowing that by doing so *in accordance with justice* he serves the whole of society" (quoted in Clark 1984: 68).

The plebeian radical William Benbow originated the idea of the General Strike — the "Grand National Holiday" of the working classes — in 1832 (Benbow n.d.). (The Dean is wrong when he writes that anarcho-syndicalism "can be traced back, in fact, to notions of a 'Grand Holiday' [*sic*] or general strike proposed by the English Chartists" (7). Although Benbow went on to become a Chartist, there was no Chartist movement in 1832, the Chartists never espoused the general strike, and there was never anything remotely syndicalist about the Chartists' purely political program centered on universal male suffrage [Black 1996c].) Benbow called upon the direct producers "to establish the happiness of the *immense majority* of the human race" — namely, themselves — to secure their own "ease, gaiety, pleasure and happiness." If it's hedonistic or decadent for impoverished, exploited, overworked people to stage a revolution for generalized case, gaiety, pleasure and happiness, long live hedonism and decadence!

The Dean's yapping about "Yuppie" self-indulgence is, even aside from its gross hypocrisy, misdirected. The problem is not that Yuppies, or unionized factory workers, or small businessmen, or retirees, or whomever, are selfish. In an economy orchestrated by scarcity and risk, where almost anybody might be "downsized" (Black 1996b), only the super-rich can afford *not* to be selfish (but they usually are anyway: old habits die hard). The problem is the prevailing *social organization of selfishness* as a divisive force which actually diminishes the self. As society is now set up, individual selfishness is collectively, and literally, *self*-defeating.

The Dean recoils in horror from a coinage he attributes to Hakim Bey, "Marxism-Stirnerism" (20) — actually, as Bookchin probably knows, Bey borrowed it from me (Black 1986: 130). It comes from my Preface to the Loompanics reprint of a pro-situationist text, *The Right to Be Greedy* (For Ourselves 1983), which argued for "communist egoism." I made it clear that I didn't think the essay offered any ultimate resolution of the tension between the individual the social. No theory will ever accomplish that *a priori*, although theory might inform its resolution in practice. But the essay is acute in distinguishing the self-sacrificing militant from the selfish revolutionary: "Any revolutionary who is to be counted upon can only be in it for *himself* — unselfish people can always switch loyalty from one projection to another" (For Ourselves 1983) — for example, from Stalinism to Trotskyism to Anarchism to....

We need, not for people to be less selfish, but for us to be better at *being* selfish in the most effective way, together. For that, they need to understand themselves and society better — to desire better, to enlarge their perceptions of the genuinely possible, and to appreciate the real institutional (and ideological) impediments to realizing their real desires. By "real desires" I don't mean "what I want people to want," I mean what *they* really want, severally and together, as arrived at — as Benbow so presciently put it — by unconstrained, general, unhurried reflection, "to get rid of our ignorant impatience, and to learn what it is we do want." And also what we "do *not* need" (Bookchin 1977: 307).

In typical retro-Marxist fashion, the Dean purports to resort, on this point as on others, to the ultimate argument from authority, the argument from History:

The Austrian workers' uprising of February 1934 and the Spanish Civil War of 1936, *I can attest* [emphasis added], were more than orgiastic "moments of insurrection" but were bitter struggles carried on with desperate earnestness and magnificent elan, all aesthetic epiphanies notwithstanding (23).

As a preliminary quibble — I can sometimes be as petty as lit. Dean usually is — I object to the word "attest" here. To "attest" to something — the signing of a will, for instance — means to affirm it as a witness, from personal knowledge. Bookchin was 13 in 1934 and 15 in 1936. He has no more personal knowledge of either of these revolts than my six year old niece does. Similarly, the Dean "would like to recall a Left That Was," "the Left of the nineteenth and early twentieth century" (66), and rattles away as if he were doing exactly that — although that is, for someone born in 1921, a chronological impossibility. Another old man, Ronald Reagan, remembered the moving experience of liberating German concentration camps, although he spent World War II making propaganda films in Hollywood. What the uprising of the Austrian workers (state socialists, incidentally, not anarchists), savagely suppressed in only three days, has to do with present-day revolutionary anarchist prospects, I have no more idea than Bookchin seems to. Abstaining from "orgiastic" insurrection, if they did, must not have improved their military situation much.

Spain, where anarchists played so prominent a role in the revolution, especially in its first year, is a more complicated story. *Of course* it was a bitter struggle. It was a war, after all, and war is hell. Hey! — this just occurred to me — did Bookchin fight the Fascists when *he* had the *chancy* in World War II? Not that I've ever heard. He would have been draft-age military material, at age 21, in 1942 when they were drafting almost everybody, even my spindly, nearsighted 30 year old father. Waving the bloody shirt at lifestyle anarchists might be more impressive if Bookchin had ever worn it.

The fact that an experience is *one* thing doesn't necessarily entail that it is *only* that one thing. This is the sort of metaphysical dualism which vitiates almost everything the Dean has to say (Jarach 1996). There was a great deal festivity and celebration even in the Spanish Revolution, despite the unfavorable conditions. In Barcelona, "there was a festive enthusiasm in the streets" (Fraser 1979:152). Some couples, "'believing the revolution made everything possible' began living together and splitting up with too much ease (*ibid*.: 223). George Orwell, who fought with them, reported that the Catalan militiamen on the Aragon front were badly armed and even water was scarce, but "there was plenty of wine" (1952: 32). Indeed, "Orwell's description of the city [of Barcelona] during this phase is still intoxicating: the squared and avenues bedecked with black-and-red flags, the armed people, the slogans, the stirring revolutionary songs, the feverish enthusiasm of creating a new world, the gleaming hope, and the inspired heroism" (Bookchin 1977: 306). In Barcelona, young anarchists commandeered cars — motoring was a thrill hitherto beyond their means — and careened through the streets on errands of dubious revolutionary import (Seidman 1991: 1, 168; Borkenau 1963: 70): mostly they were just joyriding. Bookchin reviles the romanticism of the lifestyle anarchists, forgetting his own statement that "Spanish Anarchism placed a strong emphasis on life-style" (1977: 4). As José Peirats remembered the Spanish Revolution, "we regarded ourselves as the last romantics" (Bolloten 1991: 769 n. 17). May they not be the last!

Consider the Paris Commune of 1871, which the Situationists referred to as the greatest rave-up of the nineteenth century:

The Communards of the Belleville district in Paris, who fought the battles of the barricades and died by the tens of thousands under the guns of the Versaillais, refused to confine their insurrection to the private world described by symbolist poems or the public world described by Marxist economics. They demanded the eating and the moral, the filled belly and the heightened sensibility. The Commune floated on a sea of alcohol — for weeks everyone in the Belleville district was magnificently drunk. Lacking the middle-class proprieties of their instructors, the Belleville Communards turned their insurrection into a festival of public joy, play and solidarity (Bookchin 1971: 277).

Revolutionaries make love *and* war.

Chapter 4: On Organization

Well, *finally,* the Dean has identified a concrete "programmatic" difference between him and his appointed enemies. Most, maybe all of those he criticizes as "lifestyle anarchists" indeed oppose the establishment of some sort of authoritative anarchist organization, as well they should (Black 1992:1 181–193). It is something North American anarchists have always shied away from, even in the heyday of the Left That Was. The Dean, as previously noted, has spent his entire anarchist life going out of his way not to involve himself with any such organization — not from principle, apparently, but because he was preoccupied, personalistically, with his own career. Some of us think the enterprise is ill-advised, even counterproductive, even apart from our suspicion that it wouldn't advance *our* careers. A lot of us don't even *have* careers.

Jacques Camatte (1995: 19–38) and, before him, the disillusioned socialist Robert Michels (1962) with whom the Dean is not entirely unfamiliar (1987: 245), provided some theoretical reasons for us to think so. Dean Bookchin himself (1977,1996) recounts the bureaucratic degeneration of what he considers the greatest anarcho-syndicalist organization of them all, the Spanish CNT-FAI. Even Kropotkin, one of the few anarchists to enjoy the Dean's imprimatur, thought that a syndicalist regime would be far too centralized and authoritarian: "As to its Confederal Committee, it borrows a great deal too much from the Government that it has just overthrown" (1990: xxxv).

With organizations, especially large-scale ones, the means tend to displace the ends; the division of labor engenders inequality of power, officially or otherwise; and representatives, by virtue of greater interest, experience, and access to expertise, effectively supplant those they represent. We agree with the Dean that "the words 'representative democracy,' taken literally, are a contradiction in terms" (1987: 245). In other words, "delegated authority entails hierarchy" (Dahl 1990: 72). Thus in Spain the 30,000 *faistas* quickly came to control one million *cenetistas*, whom they led into policies — such as entering the government — to which the FAI militants should have been even more fiercely opposed than the rank-and-file CNT unionists. In a crisis — which might be of their own creation — the leadership generally consults its "personalistic" interests and the maintenance requirements of the organization, in that order; only then, if ever, their announced ideology; not the will of the membership (although the leaders will invoke it if it happens to coincide with their policies and, for that matter, even if it doesn't). This has happened too often to be an accident.

We do not reject organization because we are ignorant of the history of anarchist organizations. We reject it, among other reasons, because we know that history only too well, and Bookchin is one of those who has taught it to us. Nobody is surprised that business corporations, government bureaucracies, hieratic churches and authoritarian political parties are in practice, as in theory, inimical to liberty, equality and fraternity. (Also incompetent: as Paul Goodman put it [1994: 58], central organization "mathematically guarantees stupidity.") What at first surprises, and what cries out for explanation, is that egalitarian and libertarian organizations sooner or later — usually sooner — end up the same way.

Robert Michels (himself a socialist) studied the German Social Democratic Party — a Marxist party programmatically committed to social equality — a few years before the First World War, and found it to be thoroughly hierarchic and bureaucratic. Vindicating Michels, the vast majority of German socialists, contrary to their official antiwar position, promptly followed their leaders in supporting the war. Anarchists might congratulate themselves that Marxism, unlike anarchism, was a "bourgeois ideology" (Bookchin 1979) — like the Pharisees, thanking God that they are not as other men. (Although that would be "idealism," another bourgeois ideology.) Michels, writing at a time when syndicalism seemed to be an important social movement, noted:

Here we find a political school, whose adherents are numerous, able, well-educated, and generous-minded, persuaded that in syndicalism it has discovered the antidote to oligarchy. But we have to ask whether the antidote to the oligarchical tendencies of organization can possibly be found in a method which is itself rooted in the principle of representation.... Syndicalism is... mistaken in attributing to parliamentary democracy alone the inconveniences that arise from the principle of delegation in general (1962: 318).

Bob Black

Times have changed: North American syndicalists aren't numerous, aren't able, and least of all are they generous-minded, although most may be "well-educated" if you equate a good education with college — something that I, having taught American college students, don't do.

The Spanish experience suggests that Michels was right about "organization" at least in the sense of large-scale organizations whose higher reaches consist of representatives, such as the Spanish CNT or the confederal "Commune of communes" (57) the Dean desires. Even if these organizations are only minimally bureaucratic — a precious, and precarious, accomplishment — they are nonetheless inherently hierarchic. The CNT pyramid had at least six levels (and some outbuildings):

Section → Syndicate → Local federation of syndicates → Comercal federation → Regional confederation → National confederation (congress) (Brademas 1953: 16–17)

This leaves out, for instance, several intermediary bodies such as the Regional Plenum, the Plenum of Regionals (no, I'm *not* joking) and the National Committee (Bookchin 1977: 170). What happened was just what might have been expected to happen had anybody anticipated the CNT's abrupt rise to power. When their turn came, in Spain, the organizational anarchists blew it too. It is not only that the most vociferous FAI militants, like Montseney and García Oliver, joined the Loyalist government — that could be explained away, albeit implausibly, as "personalistic" treachery — but that most of the CNT-FAI rank-and-file went along with it (Brademas 1953: 353). Even more startling than the leaders' support for what they were supposed to be against (the state) was their opposition to what they were supposed to be for — social revolution — which swept over much of Republican Spain without the support, and in most cases over the objections, of the leaders (Bolloten 1991; Broué & Témime 1972). The leaders placed the war ahead of the revolution and managed, at the cost of a million lives, to lose both (Richards 1983).

The Spanish experience was not unique. The Italian syndicalists mostly went over to Fascism (Roberts 1979). The sham industrial democracy of syndicalist corporatism only needed a little fine-tuning and a touch of cosmetics to be finessed into the sham syndicalism of Fascist corporatism.

For North Americans, no example — not even the Spanish example — is more important than the Mexican Revolution. Had it turned out differently, it would have recoiled upon the United States with incalculable force. Because the revolution was contained south of the border, in America the Federal and state governments (and the vigilantes they encouraged) had a free hand to crush the anarchists, syndicalists and socialists so thoroughly that they've never recovered.

During the Mexican Revolution, the organized anarcho- syndicalists supported the liberals — the Constitutionalists — *against* the Zapatista and Villista social revolutionaries (Hart 1978: ch. 9). As urban rationalist progressives (like Bookchin), they despised peasant revolutionaries still clinging to Catholicism. Besides, they thought that Pancho Villa — *here's* an uncanny precursor to Bookchinist jargon — acted too much like a "personalist"! (*ibid.*: 131). On behalf of the Constitutionalist regime — the one President Wilson sent the U.S. Army in to prop up — the anarcho-syndicalists raised "Red Battalions," perhaps 12,000 strong, "a massive augmentation of commanding general Obregon's Constitutional army" (*ibid.*: 133, 135). They soon reaped the reward — repression — that they'd earned. By 1931 the government had the Mexican working class under control (*ibid.*: 175–177, 183), as it still does. If revolution resumes it will be the *Neo*-Zapatistas, the Mayan peasants of Chiapas, who set it off (Zapatistas 1994).

Without attempting a comprehensive critique of the Dean's municipal-confederal socialism, I'd like to raise a couple of prosaic points of fact which do not depend upon, although they are consistent with, the anti-organizational critiques of Michels, Camatte, Zerzan, myself and, by now, many others. Direct democracy is not, and for all anybody knows, never was, all it's cracked up to be by the Dean. Most of the extant authors from classical antiquity, who knew the working system better than we ever will, were anti-democratic (Finley 1985: 8–11), as Bookchin elsewhere admits (1989: 176). The word "democracy" was almost always used pejoratively before the nineteenth century — that is, when it referred only to direct democracy: "To dismiss this unanimity as a debasement of the currency, or to dismiss the other side of the debate as apologists who misuse the term, is to evade the need for explanation" (Finley 1985: 11; cf. Bailyn 1992: 282–285).

The Athenian *polis*, the most advanced form of direct democracy ever practiced for any extended period, was oligarchic. It's not only that, as Bookchin grudgingly concedes (59), the polity excluded slaves, numerous other noncitizens (one-third of free men were technically foreigners [Walzer 1970: 106]), and women, *i.e.,* the *polis* excluded the overwhelming majority of adult Athenians. Even the Dean acknowledges, but attaches no importance to, the fact that maybe three-fourths of adult male Athenians were "slaves and disenfranchised resident aliens" (1987: 35). It could not have been otherwise:

These large disenfranchised populations provided the material means for many Athenian male citizens to convene in popular assemblies, function as mass juries in trials, and collectively administer the affairs of the community (Bookchin 1989: 69).

"A modicum of free time was needed to participate in political affairs, leisure that was probably [!] supplied by slave labour, although it is by no means true that all active Greek citizens were slave owners" (Bookchin 1990: 8). Greek culture, as Nietzsche observed, flourished at the expense of the "overwhelming majority": "At their expense, through their extra work, that privileged class is to be removed from the struggle for existence, in order to produce and satisfy a new world of necessities" (1994: 178).

There are two more points to ponder.

The first is that the vast majority of the Athenian citizen minority abstained from participation in direct democracy, just as the majority of American citizens abstain from our representative democracy. Up to 40,000 Athenian men enjoyed the privilege of citizenship, less than half of whom resided in the city itself (Walzer 1970: 17). "All the policy decisions of the *polis*," according to Bookchin, "are formulated directly by a popular assembly, or *Ecclesia*, which every male citizen from the city and its environs (Attica) is expected to attend" (1974: 24). In reality, the facility provided for the assembly accommodated only a fraction of them (Dahl 1990: 53–54), so most must have been expected *not* to attend, and didn't. Attendance probably never exceeded 6,000, and was usually below 3,000. The only known tally of the total vote on a measure is 3,461 (Zimmern 1931: 169). And this despite the fact that many citizens were slaveowners who were thereby relieved, in whole or in part, of the need to work (Bookchin 1990: 8). And despite the fact that the prevalent ideology, which even Socrates subscribed to, "emphatically prioritized the social over the individual," as the Dean approvingly asserts that Bakunin did (5): "as a matter of course," the Athenians "put the city first and the individual nowhere" (Zimmern 1931: 169–170 n. 1). Even most Athenians with the time to spare for public affairs avoided political involvement.

In this respect they resembled the remnants of direct democracy in America, the New England town meetings. These originated in the Massachusetts Bay colony when the dispersal of settlements made a unitary central government impractical. At first informally, but soon formally, towns exercised substantial powers of self-government. The original form of self-government was the town meeting of all freemen, which took place anywhere from weekly to monthly. This system still prevails, formally, in some New England towns, including those in Bookchin's adopted state Vermont — but as a form without content. In Vermont the town meeting takes place only one day a year (special meetings are possible, but rare). Attendance is low, and declining: "In recent years there has been a steady decline in participation until in some towns there are scarcely more persons present than the officials who are required to be there" (Nuquist 1964: 4–5). The Dean has thrown a lot of fairy-dust on present-day Vermont town meetings (1987:268–270; 1989: 181) without ever claiming that they play any real role in governance. Indeed, Bookchin hails the town meeting's "control" (so-called) precisely *because* "it does not carry the ponderous weight of law" (1987: 269): in other words, it's just a populist ritual. By failing to either "carry the ponderous weight of law" or jettison it — tasks equally beyond its illusory authority — the town meeting legitimates those who do carry, willingly, the ponderous weight of law, the practitioners of what the Dean calls statecraft.

In modern Vermont as in ancient Athens, most people think they have better things to do than attend political meetings, because most people are not political militants like the Dean. Several sorts of, so to speak, special people flock to these get-togethers. These occasions tend to attract a person (typically a man) who is an ideological fanatic, a control freak, an acting-out victim of mental illness, or somebody who just doesn't have a life, and often someone favored by some combination of the foregoing civic virtues.

Face-to-face democracy is in-your-face democracy. To the extent that the tireless typicals turn up, they discourage those not so afflicted from participating actively or returning the next time. The Dean, for instance, speaks glowingly of "having attended many town meetings over the last fifteen years" (1987: 269) — they aren't even held where he lives Burlington — who but a political pervo-voyeur could possibly get off on these solemn ceremonies? Some people like to watch autopsies too. The same types who'd get themselves elected in a representative democracy tend to dominate, by their bigmouthed bullying, a direct democracy too (Dahl 1990: 54). Normal non-obsessive people will often rather appease the obsessives or even kick them upstairs than prolong an unpleasant interaction with them. If face-to-face democracy means having to face democrats like Bookchin, most people would rather execute an about-face. And so the minority of political obsessives, given an institutional opportunity, tend to have their way. That was how it was in Athens, where direction came from what we might call militants, what they called demagogues: "demagogues — I use the word in a neutral sense — were a structural element in the Athenian political system [which] could not function without them" (Finley 1985: 69).

In "A Day in the Life of a Socialist Citizen," Michael Walzer (1970: ch. 11) sent up muscular, direct democracy before Bookchin publicized his version of it. Walzer's point of departure was what Marx and Engels wrote in *The German Ideology* about how the post-revolutionary communist citizen is a fully realized, all-sided person who "hunts in the morning, fishes in the afternoon, rears cattle in the evening, and plays the critic after dinner" without ever being confined to any or all of these social roles (*ibid.*: 229). Bookchin has endorsed this vision (1989: 192, 195). Sounds good, but a muscular municipal socialist has further demands on his time:

Before hunting in the morning, this unalienated man of the future is likely to attend a meeting of the Council on Animal Life, where he will be required to vote on important matters relating to the stocking of the forests. The meeting will probably not end much before noon, for among the many-sided citizens there will always be a lively interest even in highly technical problems. Immediately after lunch, a special session of the Fishermen's Council will be called to protest the maximum catch recently voted by the Regional Planning Commission, and the Marxist man will participate eagerly in these debates, even postponing a scheduled discussion of some contradictory theses on cattle-rearing. Indeed he will probably love argument far better than hunting, fishing, *or* rearing cattle. The debates will go on so long that the citizens will have to rush through dinner in order to assume their role as critics. Then off they will go to meetings of study groups, clubs, editorial boards, and political parties where criticism will be carried on long into the night (*ibid.*: 229–230).

In other words, "Socialism means the rule of the men with the most evenings to spare" (*ibid.*: 235). Walzer is far from being my favorite thinker (Black 1985), but what he sketched here is as much paradigm as parody. It scarcely exaggerates and in no way contradicts Rousseau's — his fellow Genevan Calvin's — ascetic republican civism, which in turn is disturbingly close to Bookchin's muscular, moralistic municipalism.

The Dean has long insisted upon the potential of what he calls "liberatory technology" to free the masses from toil and usher in a post-scarcity society (1971: 83–139). "Without major technological advances to free people from toil," anarchy — especially "primitivistic, prerational, antitechnological, and anticivilizational" anarchy — is impossible (26). No part of his Marxist heritage is more vital to Bookchin than its notion of humanity passing from the realm of necessity to the realm of freedom by way of the rational, socially responsible application of the advanced technology created by capitalism.

The Dean is furious with "lifestyle anarchists" who doubt or deny this postulate of positivist progressivism, but for present purposes, let's assume he's right. Let's pretend that under anarcho-democratic, rational control, advanced technology would drastically reduce the time devoted to production work and afford economic security to all. Technology would thus do for the upright (and uptight) republican Bookchinist citizenry what slavery and imperialism did for the Athenian citizenry — *but no more*. Which is to say, not nearly enough.

For even if technology reduced the hours of work, it would not reduce the hours in a day. There would still be 24 of them. Let's make-believe we could automate *all* production-work away. Even if we did, technics couldn't possibly do more than shave a few minutes off the long hours which deliberative, direct democracy would necessitate, the "often prosaic, even tedious but most important forms of self-management that required patience, commitment to democratic procedures, lengthy debates, and a decent respect for the opinions of others within one's community" (Bookchin 1996: 20; cf. Dahl 1990: 32–36, 52). (I pass over as beneath comment Bookchin's avowal of "a decent respect for the opinions of others.") Having to race from meeting to meeting to try to keep the militants from taking over would be even worse than working, but without the pay.

That was the first practical objection. The second is that there is no reason to believe that there has ever *been* an urban, purely direct democracy or even a reasonable approximation of one. Every known instance has involved a considerable admixture of representative democracy which sooner or later usually subordinated direct democracy where it didn't eliminate it altogether. In Athens, for instance, a Council of 500, chosen monthly by lot, set the agenda for the meetings of the *ekklesia* (there was no provision for new business to be brought up from the floor [Bookchin 1971: 157; Zimmern 1931: 170 n. 1]) and which, in turn, elected an inner council of 50 for governing between assemblies, which in turn elected a daily chairman. Sir Alfred Zimmern, whose sympathetic but dated account of Athenian democracy the Dean has referred to approvingly (1971: 159, 288 n. 27), observed that the Council consisted of paid officials (Zimmern 1931: 165), a detail the Dean omits. In general, "the sovereign people judged and administered by delegating power to representatives" (*ibid,*: 166). Generals, for instance — very important officials in an imperialist state frequently at war — were *elected* annually (Dahl 1990: 30; cf. Bookchin 1971: 157). These were remarkably radical democratic institutions for their day, and even for ours, but they are also substantial departures from Bookchinist direct democracy. Nonetheless the Dean only grudgingly admits that Athens was even a "*quasi*-state" (Bookchin 1989: 69), whatever the hell a "*quasi*-state," is. Unbelievably, the Dean claims that "Athens had a 'state' in a very limited and piecemeal sense... the 'state' as we know it in modern times could hardly be said to exist among the Greeks" (1987: 34). Just ask Socrates. What'll you be having? Hemlock, straight up. The Dean has elsewhere explained that in his municipal Utopia, face-to-face assemblies would set policy but leave its administration to "boards, commissions, or collectives of qualified, even elected officials" (Bookchin 1989: 175) — the experts and the politicians. Again: "Given a modest but by no means small size, the *polis* could be arranged institutionally so that it could have its affairs conducted by well-rounded, publicly-engaged men with a minimal, carefully guarded degree of representation" (Bookchin 1990: 8). Meet the new boss, same as the old boss!

Consider Switzerland, a highly decentralized federal republic which for the Dean is a fascinating example of "economic and political coordination within and between communities that render[s] statecraft and the nation-state utterly superfluous" (1987: 229). Alexis de Tocqueville, as astute a student of democracy as ever was, wrote in 1848:

It is not sufficiently realized that, even in those Swiss cantons where the people have most preserved the exercise of their power, there does exist a representative body entrusted with some of the cares of government. Now, it is easy to see, when studying recent Swiss history, that gradually those matters with which the people concern themselves are becoming fewer, whereas those with which their representatives deal are daily becoming more numerous and more important. Thus the principle of pure democracy is losing ground gained by the opposing principle. The former is insensibly becoming the exception and the latter the rule (1969b: 740).

Even in the Swiss cantons there were representative bodies (legislatures) to which the executive and the judiciary were strictly subordinate (*ibid.*: 741). Civil liberties were virtually unknown and civil rights entirely so, a much worse situation than in most European monarchies at the time (*ibid.*: 738). De Tocqueville considered the Swiss Confederation of his day "the most imperfect of all the constitutions of this kind yet seen in the world" (*ibid.*: 744). Earlier, John Adams had also made the point that the Swiss cantons were aristocratic republics as well as observing that their historical tendency was for hereditary elites to entrench themselves in office (Coulborn 1965: 101–102).

As for the "economic and political coordination" which renders the Swiss "nation-state utterly superfluous" (Bookchin 1987: 229), if the Swiss nation-state is *utterly* superfluous, why does it exist at all? As it does, as surely as exist the Swiss banks whose numbered accounts safeguard so much of the loot of the world's dictators and gangsters (Ruwart 1996: 4). Is there possibly a connection? Might Switzerland's rakeoff from loan-sharking and money-laundering underwrite its direct democracy (such as it is) just as slavery and imperialism underwrote the direct democracy of Athens? A Swiss parliamentarian once referred to his country as a nation of receivers of stolen goods.

Those of us who are somewhat older than most North American anarchists, although much younger than the Dean, also recall the history of efforts to form an all-inclusive anarchist organization here. Never did they come close to success. (To anticipate an objection — the Industrial Workers of the World is not now, and never has been, an avowedly anarchist organization. It is syndicalist, not anarchist [and not Bookchinist]). Not until about 1924, when most of the membership had fallen away, joined the Communist Party, or in some cases gone to prison, was the little that was left of the One Big Union essentially, if unofficially, an anarchist organization.) Much later the Anarchist Communist Federation made an effort to unify the workerist/organizational anarchists, and most recently the ex- (or maybe not so ex-) Marxists around *Love & Rage*, whose anarchist bona fides are widely doubted, flopped too.

At this time there seems to be no interest in a continental anarchist federation. The only apparent purpose for one is to legislate standards of anarchist orthodoxy (Black 1992: 181–193), an objective understandably unwelcome to the unorthodox majority of anarchists, although that now appears to be the Dean's belated goal. While the anarchist ranks have greatly grown during the decades of decadence, we are far from numerous and united enough to assemble in a fighting organization. But no cult is ever too small for its own little Inquisition.

So, yes, we "lifestyle anarchists" tend to be anti-organizational, in the sense that we know that anarchist organizations have a poor track record and also that, given our numbers, our resources, and our differences, North American anarchists have no compelling reason to believe that what's never worked for us before would work if we tried it now. It is not as if these organizing efforts are indispensable to accomplish even what little we are already accomplishing. Mostly what we are accomplishing is publishing. After the ACF fell apart, the collective which had been responsible for producing its newspaper *Strike!* continued to do so on its own for some years. An organization may need a newspaper, but a newspaper may not need an organization (Black 1992: 192). In the case of *Love & Rage*, the newspaper preceded what little there is to its continental organization. Self-reports and other reports of anarchist burnout within leftist anti-authoritarian collectives abound (*No Middle Ground, Processed World, Open Road, Black Rose Books, Sabotage Bookstore*, etc.). These are, for anarchists, usually ideological killing-fields. Ironically, the allegedly anti-organizational collectives, such as Autonomedia and the *Fifth Estate,* have outlasted most of the organizational ones. Could it be that the organizer-types are too individualistic to get along with each other?

Chapter 5: Murray Bookchin, Municipal Statist

There is no putting off the inevitable any longer. It has to be said: Dean Bookchin is not an anarchist. By this I do *not* mean that he is not *my* kind of anarchist, although that too is true. I mean he is not *any* kind of anarchist. The word means something, after all, and what it means is denial of the necessity and desirability of government. That's a bare- bones, pre-adjectival definition anterior to any squabbling about individualist, collectivist, communist, mutualist, social, lifestyle, ecological, mystical, rational, primitivist, Watsonian, ontological, etc. anarchisms. An anarchist as such is opposed to government — full stop. Dean Bookchin is not opposed to government. Consequently, he is not an anarchist.

What! "The foremost contemporary anarchist theorist" (Clark 1990: 102) is *not* an anarchist? You heard me. He's not — really and truly, he's not. And not because he flunks some abstruse ideological test of my own concoction. He's not an anarchist because he believes in government. An anarchist can believe in many things, and all too often does, but government is not one of them.

There's nothing heinous about not being an anarchist. Some of my best friends are not anarchists. They do not, however, claim to be anarchists, as the Dean does.

I could take some cheap shots at the Dean — come to think of it, I think I will! How many of his Red-and-Green disciples know that he was formerly in favor of a modest measure of *nuclear power?* Solar, wind, and tidal power should be exploited to the max, but "it would be impossible to establish an advanced industrial economy based exclusively on solar energy, wind power, or even tidal power" (Herber 1965: 193), and we *must* have an advanced industrial economy, that goes without saying. So, though we shouldn't "overcommit ourselves to the use of nuclear fuels," the clean energy sources will not suffice: "These gaps will be filled by nuclear and fossil fuels, but we will employ them judiciously, always taking care to limit their use as much as possible" (*ibid.*). That's a comfort.

And it would be scurrilous of me to report that this same Bookchin book (Herber 1965: ix) includes — this must be an anarchist first — a plug from a Cabinet member, then-Secretary of the Interior Stewart L. Udall: "*Crisis in Our Cities* sets forth in one volume vivid evidence that the most debilitating diseases of our time are a result of our persistent and arrogant abuse of our shared environment.... We cannot minimize the investments necessary to pollution control, but as Mr. Herber [Bookchin] documents, the penalties for not doing so have become unthinkable." This is, be it noted, a call for legislation and taxation which a closet anarchist allowed to adorn one of his books. There's also an afterword from the Surgeon General of the United States.

As embarrassing to the Dean as these reminders must be, they are not conclusive against him. It is his own explicit endorsements of the state which are decisive. Not, to be sure, the *nation-state* of modern European provenance. He doesn't like that sort of state very much. It allows for too much individual autonomy. But he is enamored of the *city-state* of classical antiquity and the occasionally, semi-self-governing "commune" of pre-industrial western Europe. In this he is reminiscent of Kropotkin, who propounded the absurd opinion that the state did not exist in western Europe prior to the sixteenth century (cf. Bookchin 1987: 33–34). That would have surprised and amused William the Conqueror and his successors, not to mention the French and Spanish monarchs and the Italian city-states familiar to Machiavelli — whose *Il Principe* was clearly not directed to a mandated and revocable delegate responsible to the base, but rather to a man on horseback, somebody like Caesare Borgia.

Although it is the most unremarkable of observations, the Dean carries on as if he's genuinely incensed that John Zerzan, reviewing his *The Rise of Urbanization and the Decline of Citizenship* (1987), pointed out that the romanticized classical Athenian *polis* has "long been Bookchin's model for a revitalization of urban politics," a "canard" to which the Dean indignantly retorts, "In fact, I took great pains to indicate the failings of the Athenian *polis* (slavery, patriarchy, class antagonisms, and war)" (59). He may have *felt* great pains at getting caught, but he *took* very few. The Dean made, "in fact," all of two references — not even to slavery as a mode of production, as a social reality, but to *attitudes* toward slavery (1987: 83, 87), as if the fact that classical cities had mostly subject populations (Dahl 1990: 1) was the accidental result of some collective psychic quirk, some strange thousand-year head-trip. What Zerzan said is only what one of the Dean's admirers put in stronger terms: "Bookchin continually exhorts us to hearken back to the Greeks, seeking to recapture the promise of classical thought and to comprehend the truth of the Polis" (Clark 1982: 52; Clark 1984: 202–203).

Every historian knows that large-scale slavery was a necessity for the classical city (Finley 1959), although the Dean has issued the fiat that "the image of Athens as a slave economy which built its civilization and generous humanistic outlook on the backs of human chattels is false" (1972: 159). (M.I. Finley — like the Dean, an ex-Communist [Novick 1988: 328] — is a Bookchin-approved historian [1989: 178].) Some of what Zerzan writes about paleolithic society may be conjectural and criticizable, but what he writes about Bookchin is pure reportage. The Dean plainly says that "later ideals of citizenship, even insofar as they were modeled on the Athenian, seem more unfinished and immature than the original — hence the very considerable discussion I have given to the Athenian citizen and his context" (1987: 83). That is perhaps because the even more unfinished and immature realizations of "later ideals" lacked the combination of the immense slave infrastructure and the tributary empire possessed by classical Athens. Similar paeans to Athenian citizenship pepper the Dean's early books too (1972: 155–159; 1974: ch. 1). Manifestly what's put a bee in Bookchin's beret is that Zerzan has had the temerity to *read* Bookchin's books, not just revere their distinguished author, and Zerzan has actually kept track of what the Dean's been reiterating all these years. The down side of being "arguably the most prolific anarchist writer" (Ehrlich 1996: 384) is that you leave a long paper trail.

Bookchin is a statist: a city-statist. A city-state is not an anti-state. Contemporary Singapore, for instance, is a highly authoritarian city-state. The earliest states, in Sumer, were city-states. The city is where the state originated. The ancient Greek cities were all states, most of them not even democratic states in even the limited Athenian sense of the word. Rome went from being a city-state to an empire without ever being a nation-state. The city-states of Renaissance Italy were states, and only a few of them, and not for long, were in any sense democracies. Indeed republican Venice, whose independence lasted the longest, startlingly anticipated the modern police-state (Andrieux 1972: 45–55).

Taking a worldwide comparative-historical perspective, the pre-industrial city, unless it was the capital of an empire or a nation-state (in which case it was directly subject to a resident monarch) was always subject to an oligarchy. There has never been a city which was not, or which was not part of, a state. And there has never been a state which was not a city or else didn't incorporate one or more cities. The pre-industrial city (what Gideon Sjoberg calls — a poor choice of words — the "feudal city") was the antithesis of democracy, not to mention anarchy:

Central to the stratification system that pervades all aspects of the feudal city's social structure — the family, the economy, religion, education, and so on — is the pre-eminence of the political organization.... We reiterate: the feudal, or preindustrial civilized, order is dominated by a small, privileged upper stratum. The latter commands the key institutions of the society. Its higher echelons are most often located in the capital, the lower ranks residing in the smaller cities, usually the provincial capitals (Sjoberg 1960: 220).

Sjoberg anticipated the objection, "What about Athens?" He wrote, "although the Greek city was unique for its time, in its political structure it actually approximates the typical preindustrial city far more than it does the industrial-urban order" (*ibid.*: 236). Only a small minority of Athenians were citizens, and many of them were illiterate and/or too poor to be able to participate effectively, if at all, in politics (*ibid.*: 235). Then and there, as always in cities everywhere, politics was an elite prerogative. The "latent" democracy of any and every urban republic (59) is something only Bookchin can see, just as only Wilhelm Reich could see orgones under the microscope.

Bob Black

The distinction the Dean tries to draw between "politics" mid "statecraft" (1987: 243 & *passim*) is absurd and self-serving, not to mention that it's a major mutilation of ordinary English. Even if local politics is a kinder, gentler version of national politics, it is still politics, which has been well if cynically defined as who gets what, when, where, how (Lasswell 1958).

It's not just that the Dean uses an idiosyncratic terminology to reconcile (in a ramshackle sort of a way) anarchy with democracy, he's more apoplectic than anybody could have ever thought otherwise:

Even democratic decision-making is jettisoned as authoritarian. "Democratic rule is still rule," [L. Susan] Brown warns.... Opponents of democracy as "rule" to the contrary notwithstanding, it describes the *democratic* dimension of anarchism as a majoritarian administration of the public sphere. Accordingly, Communalism seeks freedom rather than autonomy in the sense that I have counterpoised them (17, 57).

Moving along from his mind-boggling deduction that democracy is *democratic,* Bookchin further fusses that "pejorative words like *dictate* and *rule* properly refer to the silencing of dissenters, not to the exercise of democracy" (18). Free speech is a fine thing, but it's not democracy. You can have one without the other. The Athenian democracy that the Dean venerates, for instance, democratically silenced the dissenter Socrates by putting him to death.

Anarchists "jettison" democratic decision-making, not because it's authoritarian, but because it's statist. "Democracy" means "rule by the people." "Anarchy" means "no rule." There are two different words because they refer to (at least) two different things.

I don't claim — and to make my point, I don't have to claim — that the Dean's characterization of anarchism as generalized direct democracy has no basis whatsoever in traditional anarchist thought. The anarchism of some of the more conservative classical anarchists is indeed along these lines — although Bookchin's version, right down to such details as its philhellenism, is instead an unacknowledged appropriation from the avowedly anti-anarchist Hannah Arendt

(1958). Ironically, it is the anarchists Bookchin disparages as individualists — like Proudhon and Goodman — who best represent this anarchist theme. It was the individualist egoist Benjamin Tucker who defined an anarchist as an "unterrified Jeffersonian democrat." But another theme with as least as respectable an anarchist pedigree holds that democracy is not an imperfect realization of anarchy but rather statism's last stand. Many anarchists believe, and many anarchists have always believed, that democracy is not just a grossly deficient version of anarchy, it's not anarchy at all. At any rate, no "direct face-to-face democracy" (57) that I am aware of has delegated to comrade Bookchin (mandated, revocable, and responsible to the base) the authority to pass or fail anarchists which he enjoys to pass or fail college students.

It is by no means obvious, and the Dean nowhere demonstrates, that local *is* kinder and gentler — not where local refers to local *government*. It is equally as plausible that, as James Madison argued, a large and heterogeneous polity is more favorable to liberty than the "small republic," as then local minorities can find national allies to counteract local majoritarian tyranny (Cooke 1961: 351–353). But after all, as he says himself, the Dean isn't interested in liberty (in his jargon, autonomy [57],) but only in what he calls social freedom, the participatory, self-ratified servitude of indoctrinated moralists to the petite polity in which they function as self-effacing citizen-units.

My present purpose is not to take the full measure of Bookchinism, only to characterize it as what it manifestly is, as an ideology of government — democracy — not a theory of anarchy. Bookchin's "minimal agenda" — this hoary Marxist word "minimal" is his, not mine (1987: 287) — is unambiguously statist, not anarchist. The "fourfold tenets," the Four Commandments he requires all anarchists to affirm, although most of them do not, and never did, are:

...a confederation of decentralized municipalities; an unwavering opposition to statism; a belief in direct democracy; and a vision of a libertarian communist society (60).

By some quirk of fate, Bookchin's minimal, believe-it-or-else anarchist creed just happens to be *his* creed. It also happens to be deliriously incoherent. A "confederation of decentralized municipalities" contradicts "direct democracy," as a confederation is at best a representative, not a direct, democracy. It also contradicts "an unwavering opposition to statism" because a city-state or a federal state is still a state. And by requiring, not "a libertarian communist society," only the *vision* of one, the Dean clearly implies that there is more to such a society than obedience to the first Three Commandments — but exactly *what* more, he isn't saying. The Dean is relegating higher-stage anarchy (the real thing) to some remote future time, just as the Marxists relegate what they call higher-stage communism to some hazy distant future which seems, like a mirage, forever to recede.

Amazingly, the Dean considers a city like New York (!) to be "largely made up of neighborhoods — that is to say, largly organic communities that have a certain measure of identity" (1987: 246). (He has elsewhere and inconsistently written that the modern world "lacks real cities" [Bookchin 1974: viii].) But community "obviously means more than, say, neighborhood" (Zerzan 1994: 157) — more than mere propinquity. And obviously Bookchin's been away from his home town for an awfully long time, especially if civility and civic virtue play any part in his conception of an organic community. I wouldn't recommend he take a midnight stroll in some of these "organic communities" if he values his own organism. If the criterion of an organic community is "a certain measure of identity," many wealthy all-white suburbs qualify, although Bookchin blames them for the central city's problems (1974: 73–74). Jealously territorial and violent youth gangs are the most conspicuous manifestations of community in many impoverished and otherwise atomized New York neighborhoods, his "colorful ethnic neighborhoods" (1974: 72) of childhood memory. If racial-caste and social-class residential segregation is the Dean's idea of what defines organic communities, then organic communities certainly exist in New York City, but not many people who live in them, except the very rich, are very happy about it.

While the word "anarchism" appears on almost every page of the Dean's diatribe, the word "anarchy" rarely if ever does. The ideology, the *ism,* is what preoccupies him, not the social condition, the way of life, it's presumably supposed to guide us toward. It may not be an inadvertent choice of words that what Bookchin lays down, as one of his Four Commandments of orthodox anarchism, is "an unwavering opposition to stat*ism*" (60: emphasis added), not an unwavering opposition to the *state*. As a democrat, the Dean is at best capable of only a wavering opposition to the state, whereas an abstract rejection of an abstraction, "statism," is easy enough to issue. And I'm sure it's no accident that his shot at the mainstream marketing of Bookchinism (Bookchin 1987a) nowhere identifies the Dean as an anarchist or his teachings as any kind of anarchism.

A further Bookchinist fiddle — this one a blatant regression to Marxism (indeed, to St.-Simonianism) — is the distinction between "policy" and "administration" (*ibid.*: 247–248). Policy is made, he says, by the occasional face-to-face assembly which pushy intellectuals like Bookchin are so good at manipulating. Administration is for the experts, as in higher-stage Marxist Communism, where the "government of men" is ostensibly replaced by the "administration of things." Unfortunately it is men (and it usually still *is* men) who govern *by* administering things, and by administering people as if they were things, as governors have always governed. Policy without administration is nothing. Administration with *or* without policy is everything. Stalin the General Secretary, the administrator, understood that, which is why he triumphed over Trotsky, Bukharin and all the other policy-preoccupied politicians who perhaps possibly believed in something. "Policy" is a euphemism for law, and "administration" is a euphemism for *enforcement.*

Just *what* political practice does the eximious elder prescribe to anarchists? We know how higher-stage confederal municipalism looks — muscular mentating men massed in meetings — but what is to be done in the here and now? The Dean despises existing anarchist efforts:

The sporadic, the unsystematic, the incoherent, the discontinuous, and the intuitive supplant the consistent, purposive, organized, and rational, indeed any form of sustained or focused activity apart from publishing a "zine" or pamphlet — or burning a garbage can (51).

So we are not to publish zines and pamphlets as Bookchin used to do, nor are we to burn garbage cans. Nor are we to experience freedom in the temporary collective fraternizations Hakim Bey calls Temporary Autonomous Zones (20–26). We're supposed to get organized, but Bookchin has not indicated, not even by example, what organization we're supposed to join. What then? I

On this point the Dean, usually so verbose, is allusive and elusive. I have been unable to locate in any of his writings any formulation of the "*programmatic* as well as activist social movement" he now demands (60). What I think he *is* hinting at, with nods and winks, is participation in local electoral politics:

The municipality is a potential time bomb. To create local networks and *try to transform local institutions that replicate the State* [emphasis added] is to pick up a historic challenge — a truly political one — that has existed for centuries.... For in these municipal institutions and the changes that we can make in their structure — turning them more and more into a new public sphere — lies the *abiding* institutional basis for a grassroots dual power, a grassroots concept of citizenship, and municipalized economic systems that can be counterpoised to the growing power of the centralized Nation-State and centralized economic corporations (Bookchin 1990: 12).

When the Dean speaks of transforming *existing* local institutions, when he speaks of "the changes we can make in their structure," he can only be referring to participation in local politics as it is actually conducted in the United States and Canada — by getting elected or by getting appointed by those who've gotten themselves elected. That is exactly what the world's only Bookchinist political movement, Black Rose boss Dimitri Roussopoulos' Ecologie Montreal groupuscule (Anonymous 1996:22) has attempted, and, fortunately, failed at. You can call this anything you want to — except anarchist.

To sum up: Dean Bookchin is a statist.

Chapter 6: Reason and Revolution

The Dean denounces lifestyle anarchists for succumbing to the reactionary intellectual currents of the last quarter century, such as irrationalism (1–2, 9, 55–56 & *passim*). He laments the Stirnerist "farewell to objective reality" (53) an the disdain for "reason as such" (28). With his usual self-absorption *sans* self-awareness, Bookchin fails to notice that *he* is echoing the right-wing rhetoric which since the 60's has denounced the treason of the intellectuals, their betrayal of reason and truth. There was a time when Bookchin "dismissed out of hand" the way the "bourgeois critics" condemned 60's youth culture as "anti-rational" (1970: 51). Now he joins the neo-conservative chorus:

The sixties counterculture opened a rupture not I only with the past, but with all knowledge of the past, including its history, literature, art, and music. The young people who arrogantly refused to "trust anyone [sic] over thirty," to use a popular slogan of the day, severed all ties with the best traditions of the past (Bookchin 1989: 162).

("Trust no one over thirty" (to get the slogan right) — imagine how much *that* must have irked Ye Olde Dean!)

Essentially identical elegiac wails well up regularly from the conservative demi-intelligentsia, from Hilton Kramer, Norman Podhoretz, Midge Dechter, James Q. Wilson, Irving Kristol, William F. Buckley, George Will, Newt Gingrich, Thomas Sowell, William Safire, Clarence Thomas, Pat Buchanan and the Heritage Foundation crew. Every generation, once it senses that it's being supplanted by the next one, forgets that it was once the upstart (the right-wing version) or insists that it still is (the left-wing version).

The lifestyle anarchists are afflicted, charges the Dean, with mysticism and irrationalism. These are words he does not define but repeatedly brackets as if they had the same meaning (2, 11, 19 & *passim*). They don't.

Bob Black

Mysticism is the doctrine that it is possible, bypassing the ordinary methods of perception and cognition, to experience God/Ultimate Reality directly, unmediatedly. In this sense, it is likely that Hakim Bey qualifies as a mystic, but I can't think of anybody else on the Dean's enemies list who even comes close. There is nothing innately rational *or* irrational about mysticism. Reason-identified philosophers such as Kant, Hegel and Aristotle (the latter cited 30 times in the Dean's magnum opus [1982: 376]) maintained that there is an Ultimate Reality. If they're right, for all I know it may be accessible to what Hakim Bey calls non-ordinary consciousness (1991: 68). The "epistemological anarchist," as philosopher of science Paul Feyerabend calls himself, takes great interest in experiences "which indicate that perceptions can be arranged in highly unusual ways and that the choice of a particular arrangement as 'corresponding to reality' while not arbitrary (it almost always depends on traditions), is certainly not more 'rational' or more 'objective' than the choice of another arrangement" (1975: 189–190). All I can say for myself is that, for better or for worse, I have never had a mystical experience and, furthermore, that I do not consider the notion of ultimate or absolute reality meaningful. As I once jibed, mystics "have incommunicable insights they won't shut up about" (Black 1986: 126). Mysticism is arational, not necessarily *ir*rational.

The Dean's fervent faith in objective reality (53) has more in common with mysticism than it does with science. As mystics do, Bookchin believes there is something absolute "out there" which is accessible to direct apprehension — by "reason as such" (28) on his account, by other means according to theirs. Scientists have been disabusing themselves of such simplism for about a century. The hard sciences — starting with physics, the hardest of them all — were the first to abandon a metaphysical positivism which no longer corresponded to what scientists were really thinking and doing. The Dean was at one time vaguely I aware of this (1982: 281). The not-quite-so-scientific soft sciences with lower self-esteem were slower to renounce scientism, but by now, they have, too — they have too, because they *have* to. The rejection of positivism in social thought is no post-modernist fashion. This too began a century ago (Hughes 1961: ch. 3). The glossary to a classic contemporary textbook on social science research methods could not be more blunt: "*objectivity*. Doesn't exist. See *intersubjectivity*" (Babbie 1992: G6). Settling for intersubjective verifiability within a community of practicing scientists is actually the most *conservative* post-objectivist position currently within the range of scientific respectability (*e.g.,* Kuhn 1970).

History, the maybe-science which has always had the most ambiguous and dubious claim to objectivity, held out the longest, but no longer (Novick 1988: ch. 13). Objectivity in any absolute sense is illusory, a cult fetish, a childish craving for an unattainable certitude. Intellectuals, neurotics — *i.e.,* in a political context, ideologues — "have to do with the invisible and believe in it," they have "always kept before their eyes again an intrinsically valid importance of the object, an absolute value of it, as if the doll were not the most important thing to the child, the Koran to the Turk" (Stirner 1995: 295). In contrast, the anarchist "does not believe in any absolute truth" (Rocker 1947: 27). Nor does the scientist. Nor does the mature adult. In the novel *Seven Red Sundays,* the anarchist Samar says, "This effort to stop thinking is at base religious. It represents a faith in something absolute" (Sender 1990: 253).

If Stirner bid "farewell to objective reality," if Nietzsche held "that facts are simply interpretations" (53), they were far ahead of their times. It is by now almost trite to remark that there is "no theory-independent way to reconstruct phrases like 'really there'" (Kuhn 1970: 206; cf. Bradford 1996: 259–260). Scientists dispense with objective reality for the same reason the mathematician Laplace, as he told Napoleon, dispensed with God: there's no need for the hypothesis (cf. Bookchin 1979: 23). Reviewing two recent anthologies, *Rethinking Objectivity* (Megill 1994) and *Social Experience and Anthropological Knowledge* (Hastrup & Hervik 1994), anthropologist Jay Ruby relates that no contributor to either volume argues that "an objective reality exists outside of human consciousness that is universal" (1996: 399). Intending no humor, but unwittingly providing some at Bookchin's expense, he continues: "It is unfortunate that Megill did not seek out proponents of this position, for they can easily be found among journalists — print and broadcast, documentary filmmakers, Marxists, and the political and religious right" (*ibid.*).

Bob Black

Bookchin is not the first left-wing rationalist to be outraged by this idealist, subjectivist (etc., etc.) betrayal of muscular rationalism by what one Marxist lawyer called "fideism." But this polemical predecessor of Bookchin's — a certain Lenin — had at least a nodding acquaintance with the content of the then-new physics which was undoing fundamentalist materialism (Lenin 1950). There is no indication that Bookchin has any real grounding in science, although thirty years ago he did an adequate job of popularizing information about pollution (Herber 1963, 1965). The true believers in objectivist, matter-in-motion rationalism are usually, like Lenin and Bookchin, wordmongers — lawyers, journalists (Ruby 1996: 399), or ideologues (Black 1996a) — not scientists. They believe the more fervently because they do not understand. They cling to objective reality "with the same fear a child clutches his mother's hand" (*ibid.*: 15). As Clifford Geertz says, the objectivists are "afraid reality is going to go away unless we believe very hard in it" (quoted in Novick 1988: 552). Lenin could hardly be more indignant: "But this is all *sheer obscurantism*, out-and-out reaction. To regard atoms, molecules, electrons, etc., as an approximately true reflection in our mind of the *objectively real movement of matter* is equivalent to believing in an elephant upon which the world rests!" (1950: 361). Either these impenetrable particles are bouncing around off each other down there like billiard balls on a pool table (what a *curious* model of objective reality [Black 1996a]) or they are fantasy beings like unicorns, leprechauns and lifestyle anarchists. It's appropriate that the lawyer Lenin's critique of the physics of scientists like Mach (Lenin 1950) was answered by a scientist, a prominent astronomer who was also a prominent libertarian communist: Anton Pannekoek (1948).

Ecology is a science, but Social Ecology is to ecology what Christian Science is to science. Bookchin's academic affiliations, undistinguished as they are, and his scholarly pretensions have made some impression on some anarchists, but then again, some anarchists are all too easy to impress. According to the (Bookchinist) Institute for Social Ecology, its co-founder is an "internationally acclaimed author and social philosopher" (1995: 6). *The Ecology of Freedom* (Bookchin 1982), according to a Bookchinist, is "a work of sweeping scope and striking originality" which is "destined to become a classic of contemporary social thought" (Clark 1984: 215). How is Bookchin's scholarship regarded by actual scholars? I decided to find out.

I looked up all reviews of the Dean's books listed in the *Social Sciences Index* from April 1981 to date (June 1996). I appreciate that this is a crude and incomplete measure of his reception — it fails to pick up, for instance, two notices in the academically marginal journal *Environmental Ethics* (Watson 1995; Eckersley 1989) — but it canvasses every important journal and most of the less important ones.

There were all of two reviews of the first edition of *The Ecology of Freedom,* his *Das Kapital,* "the most important book to appear so far in the history of anarchist thought" (Clark 1984:188 n. 2). The one-page review in the *American Political Science Review,* after summarizing Bookchin's contentions, asked: "Can humanity simply be integrated into the whole [*i.e.,* Nature] without losing its distinctiveness, and can solutions to the problems of the modern world emerge in the relatively spontaneous fashion Bookchin anticipates (pp. 316–317), much as problems are dealt with by ants, bees, and beavers?" (Smith 1983: 540). There's nothing on the pages cited which has anything to do with the relatively spontaneous solution of social problems which Smith claims that Bookchin espouses. The reviewer could hardly have misunderstood Bookchin more profoundly. The Dean is frantically insistent on distinguishing humans from animals and "animality" (47–48, 50, 53, 56), especially "four-legged animality" (39) — four legs bad, two legs good! Smith — whoever he is — clearly had no clue that he was reviewing a giant work of political theory.

The seven-paragraph review in the *American Anthropologist* was surprisingly favorable. Reviewer Karen L. Field wrote:

The Ecology of Freedom unites materials from many disciplines, and no doubt specialists from each one will take Bookchin to task for occasional lapses of rigor. But despite its shortcomings, the work remains the kind of wide-ranging and impassioned synthesis that is all too rare in this age of scholarly specialization (1984: 162).

In other words, the best thing about the book — and I agree — is that it thinks big. On the other hand, "the scenario he constructs is not wholly persuasive":

The description of "organic" society draws largely on materials by Paul Radin and Dorothy Lee, and paints an overly homogenized — even sanitized — picture of preliterate peacefulness and egalitarianism; it evokes !Kung and Tasaday, but not Yanomamo and Kwakiutl. Attempting to distance himself from traditional Marxian versions of the emergence of class society, Bookchin downplays the importance of technoeconomic factors, but the corresponding emphasis he places on age stratification as the key to domination is unconvincing and suffers from such a paucity of empirical evidence that it reads at times like a "Just-So" story (*ibid.*: 161).

That the Dean is taken to task for romanticizing the primitives by an anthropologist is truly matter for mirth. Nowadays *he* takes the *anthropologists* to task for romanticizing the primitives (Chapters 8 & 9). Either the Dean has reversed himself without admitting it, or else the most favorable review he's ever received from a non-anarchist, bona fide scholar rested on a serious misreading of Bookchin's magnum opus.

And it was all downhill from there.

The one specific point brought up by Field — the Dean's unsubstantiated contention that gerontocracy was the original form of hierarchy (and still the best!) — was contested, not only by Field, but subsequently by anarchist L. Susan Brown. As a feminist, she thinks it's more plausible that the sexual division of labor, whether or not it was necessarily hierarchical, eventually turned out to be the origin of hierarchy (1993: 160–161). I tend to think so too. That she dared to criticize the Dean, and in a book from his own main publisher Black Rose Books, probably explains why she got rounded up with the *un*usual suspects (13–19) although she doesn't seem to have much else in common with them.

If the academic reception of *The Ecology of Freedom* was less than triumphal, the Dean's other books have fared worse. There were no reviews in social science journals of *Post-Scarcity Anarchism* and *The Limits of the City* when they were reprinted by Black Rose Books in 1986. There were no reviews of *The Modern Crisis* (1987), or *Remaking Society* (1989), or *The Philosophy of Social Ecology* (1990), or the revised edition of *The Ecology of Freedom* (1991), or *Which Way for the Ecology Movement?* (1993), or *To Remember Spain* (1995), or, for that matter, *Social Anarchism or Lifestyle Anarchism* (1995).

There was exactly one notice of *The Rise of Urbanization and the Decline of Citizenship* (1987a) in an social science journal, and everything about it is odd. It appeared — all two paragraphs of it — in *Orbis: A Journal of World Affairs,* a right-wing, spook-ridden foreign policy journal, although the Dean's book has nothing to do with international relations. According to the anonymous, and condescending, reviewer, Bookchin's "method is to ransack world history — more or less at random — first to show how the rise of cities has corresponded to the erosion of freedom at different times and places, then to point out how some communities have fought the trend." It's not scholarship, "scholarship, though, is not his point, or his achievement." (That's for sure.) The reviewer — as had Karen Field — expresses satisfaction at reading a book with "a real idea" for a change, even if the idea is a "slightly twisted one" (Anonymous 1988: 628). This falls somewhat short of a rave review, and it reverses the Dean's understanding of urbanism, although it comports with the title of his book (later changed to *Urbanization Without Cities,* not obviously an improvement). The reviewer takes Bookchin to be arguing that the tendency of urbanism is to diminish human freedom, although here and there communities have managed to buck the trend for awhile. But what Bookchin really contends is the opposite: that the tendency of urbanism is liberatory, although here and there the elites have managed to buck the trend for awhile. The reviewer is right about urbanization but wrong about Bookchin. He did the Dean the favor of misrepresenting him.

The Dean's own conception of reason — *dialectical* reason — would have been dismissed "out of hand," as he might say, as mystical by objective-reasonists back when there were any. Like technophilia and defamation, the "dialectical approach" (Bookchin 1987b: 3–40) is a feature of Marxism to which he has always clung stubbornly. The late Karl Popper, at one time the most prominent philosopher of science of this century, denounced dialectical reasoning, not only as mystical gibberish, but as politically totalitarian in tendency (1962). He denounced "Hegelian *dialectics*; the mystery method that replaced 'barren formal logic'" (*ibid:* 1: 28). I bring this up, not because I endorse Popper's positivism — I don't (Black 1996a) — but as a reminder that people who live in the Crystal Palace shouldn't throw stones.

I myself veto no mode of reasoning or expression, although I think some are more effective than others, especially in specific contexts. There's no such thing, for instance, as *the* scientific method; important scientific discovery rarely if ever results from following rules (Feyerabend 1975). Religious forms of expression, for instance, I've long considered especially distorting (Black 1986: 71–75), but I've also insisted, as opposed to freethinker simpletons, that important truths have been expressed in religious terms: "*God* is unreal, but [He] has real but muddled referents in lived experience" (Black 1992:222). Bookchin was formerly aware of this (1982: 195–214).

The Dean's dialectic is more than a mode of reasoning: he has a "dialectical notion of causality" (Bookchin 1989: 203). The Universe itself exhibits "an overall tendency of active, turbulent substance to develop from the simple to the complex, from the relatively homogeneous to the relatively heterogeneous, from the simple to the variegated and differentiated" (*ibid.:* 199). To evolve, that is, from primal glop to *us:* "Humanity, in effect, becomes the potential voice of a nature rendered self-conscious and self-creative" (*ibid.:* 201; cf. 1987b: 30). We are one with nature — provided we follow his package directions — and at the same time we are more natural than nature has hitherto been. Out of the evolution of consciousness emerged the consciousness of evolution and now, rational self-direction. By and through this social "second nature" — conscious humanity — the dialectic actualizes the "immanent self-directedness" (1987b: 28) of the cosmos. An "immanent world reason" is the "inherent force," "the *logos* — that impart[s] meaning and coherence to reality at all levels of existence" (Bookchin 1982: 10). Humanity's duty and destiny is to inscribe the Word on the fabric of reality. The Deanly dialectic represents the most advanced thought of, say, the fourth century B.C.

In *appearance,* it's the same old story of man's God-given mission to dominate nature (Genesis 9: 1–3): the directed evolution of an objective "ecological ethics involves human stewardship of the planet" (Bookchin 1987b: 32). But in *essence,* second nature is a moment in the development of

...a radically new "free nature" in which an emancipated humanity will become the voice, indeed the expression, of a natural evolution rendered self-conscious, caring, and sympathetic to the pain, suffering, and incoherent aspects of an evolution left to its own, often wayward, unfolding. Nature, due to human rational intervention, will thence acquire the intentionality, power of developing more complex life-forms, and capacity to differentiate itself (Bookchin 1989: 202–203).

(Query: Why is it a moral imperative to make the world more complicated than it already is?) Even today, when an unemancipated humanity "is still less than human" (*ibid.*: 202), we are well on our way to rationalizing the "often wayward" course of evolution. Thanks to biotechnology, "thousands of microorganisms and plants have been patented as well as six animals. More than 200 genetically engineered animals are awaiting patent approval at the Patent and Trademark Office" (Rifkin 1995: 119). This would seem to he fully in keeping with Bookchin's program (Eckersley 1989: 111–112). Nature finds freedom at long last in submission to its highest manifestation: *us.* Just as we not-quite-humans find freedom in submission to rational direction from the first fully human being: Murray Bookchin. To paraphrase Nietzsche, not-quite-man is something to be surpassed: a rope stretched over the abyss between all the rest of us and Murray Bookchin.

Is everybody with me? Bookchin is saying that nature isn't *actually* free when it's *really* free (where really means "what it is"), when it's out of control. That's just "negative freedom" — "a formal 'freedom *from*' — rather than [positive freedom,] a substantive freedom *to*" (4).

Bob Black

We are no longer to let Nature take its course. Nature is actually free when it's really controlled by its highest manifestation, humans. Humanity is essentially natural (nature for-itself), the rest of nature isn't (nature in-itself).

Perhaps a political analogy will help. Workers aren't actually free when they're really free, *i.e.,* uncontrolled. The working class in-itself is actually free when it's really controlled by the class for-itself, the class-conscious vanguard — workers like Bookchin was, back when he was a worker.

When he tells it the way it is, the way it "actually" is, Bookchin is irrefutable. Insofar as the evidence supports him, he is "really" right. Insofar as it does not, that is because he is, to that extent, "potentially" right. (I am using these words throughout *exactly* as Bookchin does [1987b: 27J.) Reality "is no less 'real' or 'objective' in terms of what it *could* be as well as what it is at any given moment" (*ibid.:* 203). Ancient Athens might not have been a genuine direct democracy "at any given moment" or indeed in any of its moments, but if it ever had the potential for direct democracy, then it was always actually, objectively a direct democracy. To divine this mystery is "to comprehend the truth of the Polis" (Clark 1982: 52; 1984: 202–203). The fact that the potential was never realized when Athens *was* real doesn't matter. "An oak tree objectively inheres in an acorn" (Bookchin 1987b: 35 n. 22) — thus the acorn is actually an oak — even if a squirrel eats it. To call this an "idiosyncratic use of the word I *objective*" (Eckersley 1989: 101) is putting it mildly.

You can make this same trick work for the city in the I abstract, and thus for any city: "Civilization, embodied in the city as a cultural center, is divested of its rational dimensions [by anti-civilizationists], as if the city were an unabated cancer rather than the potential sphere for universalizing human intercourse, in marked contrast to the parochial limitations of tribal and village life" (34). No matter how devastating a case is made against civilization, "to malign civilization without due recognition of its enormous potentialities for *self-conscious* freedom" is "to retreat back into the shadowy world of brutishness, when thought was dim and intellectuation [*sic*] was only an evolutionary promise" (56). (At least the brutes didn't use big words that don't exist.) Democracy "lies latent in the republic" (59), any urban republic, as it has for thousands of years (and for how many thousands more?).

With characteristic understatement, the Dean concedes that his is "a fairly unorthodox notion of reason" (1982: 10). It's Hegel's philosophy of history with an abstract Humanity replacing the World-Spirit, roughly the point reached by Feuerbach. Murray Bookchin is the world's oldest Young Hegelian. God, taught Feuerbach, is merely the essence of Man, his own supreme being, mystified. But abstract Man, countered Max Stirner, is also a mystification:

The supreme being is indeed the essence of man, but just because it is his *essence* and not he himself, it remains quite immaterial whether we see it outside him and view it as "God," or find it in him and call it "essence of man" or "man." *I* am neither God nor *man,* neither the supreme essence nor my essence, and therefore it is all one in the main whether I think of the essence as in me or outside me (1995: 34).

Hegel's Christian philosophy is developing-humanity-as-supernatural. Bookchin's Marxist philosophy is developing-humanity-as-supranatural. The difference is only terminological.

Whenever Stirner says "I" he refers to himself, Max Stirner, but only as an example. Whenever he refers to the unique one or to the ego he refers, not to an abstract individual, but to each and every individual, to himself, certainly, but also to every Tom, Dick and Murray. This is why accusing Stirner of elitism (7) is bogus. Bookchin thinks that real Humanity is still less than actually human (1989: 202). Stirner thinks that every *real* human is *more* than human(ity): "'Man' as a concept or predicate does not exhaust what you are because it has a conceptual content of its own and because it lets itself stipulate what is human, what is a 'man,' because it can be defined... But can you define yourself? Are you a concept?" (1978: 67).

Positing a human essence is unnecessary for the practice of any art or science. The indwelling essence is not discoverable by observation, experimentation, or any rational mode of inquiry. To be sure, there are those who claim to have apprehended essence directly, by non-ordinary consciousness. They're called mystics, and Professor Bookchin professes to despise them. More likely he envies the qualitative superiority of their visions. Municipal socialism has got to be as mundane as mysticism gets. As Hakim Bey writes: "In sleep we dream of only two forms of government — anarchy & monarchy.... A democratic dream? a socialist dream? Impossible" (1991: 64). The Dean is indignant at this supposed denigration of "the dreams of centuries of idealists" (21) but neglects to indicate by what muscular rationalist faculty he is privy to the dreams of the dreamers of previous centuries — a ouija board perhaps? But he may be right that Bey has underestimated how far the colonization of the unconscious may have proceeded in the case of a lifelong, elderly political militant. Bookchin may well be a counterexample to the claim by a Nietzsche commentator that "there is no such thing as a dull unconscious" (Ansell-Pearson 1994: 168). Do androids dream of electric sheep? Or as Nietzsche put it: every "thing in itself" is *stupid* (1994: 81).

Whether mystical or merely mystifying, Bookchin's conception of reason is as unreasonable as so many of its results. His latest polemic is so foolish that it invites reexamination of his previous books which mostly escaped critical attention from radicals. The accolades of liberal journalists (and they'll forget him soon enough) won't avert the serious devaluation he's called down upon himself. I once defined dialectics, unfairly, as "a Marxist's excuse when you catch him lying" (1992: 149). In this sense alone is Bookchin's reasoning dialectical. After decades of talking down to eco- hippies who disdain "all muscularity of thought" (Bookchin 1987b: 3), his own mental musculature has atrophied. This time he's bitten off more than he can gum.

Chapter 7: In Search of the Primitivists Part I: Pristine Angles

Bashing the primitivist anarchists is probably Dean Bookchin's highest priority (Anonymous 1996), because they are the excommunicate anarchists whose views are most likely to be confused with, and to compete successfully with, his own. He revels in his self-image as ecology's apostle to the anarchists, and for once, there's some truth to his messianic machismo. It was the Dean, after all, who has for so long and in so many books clamored for the restoration of "organic community," as he now shamefacedly admits (41; cf. Bookchin 1974, 1982, 1987a, 1989, 1991). Once again his embarrassment is that his readers took him at his word — an error that this reader, for one, will not repeat. These innocents never suspected that they were not supposed to learn anything about primitive societies or pre-industrial communities except what cleared Bookchinist censorship.

The Dean is so much the "irate petty bourgeois" (52) on this subject that he lashes out at the primitivists in petty, peevish ways — even for *him*. Several sources John Zerzan cites in *Future Primitive* (1994), he huffs, are "entirely absent" from its bibliography, such as "'Cohen (1974)' and 'Clark (1979)'" (62 n. 19). Zerzan cites "Cohen (1974)," not on any controversial point, but for the platitude that symbols are "essential for the development and maintenance of social order" (1994: 24) — does the Dean disagree? He never says so. "Clark (1979)" may be a misprint for "Clark (1977)," which does appear in Zerzan's bibliography (1994: 173). As the author of a book from the same publisher, Autonomedia, in the same series, I know how sloppy the production values of this amateur, all-volunteer nonprofit collective can be. Additionally, Zerzan (1996: 1) in a letter to me admits to "faulty record-keeping" and explains that the absence of the two references the Dean carps about "goes back to switching to social science-type notes — after *FE* [the *Fifth Estate*] refused to run footnotes to my articles, in the '80s."

The Dean refers to part 2, ch. 4, sec. 4 of Max Stirner's *The Ego and His Own* (64–65) although the book ends with part 2, ch. 3 (Stirner 1995: viii, 320–324). My library copy of *Post-Scarcity Anarchism* (Bookchin 1971) from Ramparts Press has a list of fifteen errata taped into it which presumably ought not to shatter the reader's "faith in [Bookchin's] research" (62 n. 19), and it is far from complete: that should be Jacques Ellul, for instance, not Jacques Elul (*ibid.*: 86). And that should be Alfred Zimmern, not Edward Zimmerman (*ibid.*: 159, 288 n. 27; cf. Zimmern 1931). Bookchin was perhaps thinking of a singer-songwriter who has interested him for decades, Bob Dylan (9), the Artist Formerly Known as Zimmerman. In an especially maladroit move, the Dean cites a favorable review of Hakim Bey's *T.A.Z.* (1991) in the *Whole Earth Review* as verifying that Bey's anarchism is a decadent, "unsavory" (20) "bourgeois form of anarchism" (22): the *Whole Earth Review* has, after all, a "yuppie clientele" (23). The back jacket blurbs for just one of the Dean's books (1987) come from such arch-yuppie publications as the *Village Voice* and *The Nation*. The inside back jacket blurb boasts that he has contributed to "many journals" including *CoEvolution Quarterly*. *CoEvolution Quarterly* was the original name of the *Whole Earth Review*.

The Dean's devotion to urbanism is an important part of his hatred of the primitive. City-statism and primitive society are mutually exclusive. What amazes is that the Dean assumes that it's the primitivists, not the city-statists, who are the presumptive heretics from anarchism — that they, not he, have some explaining to do. There has never been an anarchist city, not for more than a few months at the most, but there have been many longlasting anarchist primitive societies. Many anarchists have considered anarchy possible in urban conditions — among them the Dean's *bete noir* Hakim Bey (Black 1994: 106) — but Bookchin is the first anarchist who ever posited that anarchy is *necessarily* urban. That would have come as quite a surprise to the Makhnovist peasant guerrillas in the Ukraine or the insurrectionary anarchist villagers in the *pueblos* of Andalusia (Bookchin 1977: ch. 5). My point is not that the efforts and experiences of urban anarchists are irrelevant or unworthy of attention — after all, I'm an urban anarchist myself — only that they are not the *only* anarchist experiences worthy of attention. I fail to understand why anarchists should attend only to their failures and ignore their only successes.

I don't consider myself a primitivist. Genuine anarcho-primitivists such as John Zerzan, George Bradford and Feral Faun probably don't think I'm one of them either, any more than Hakim Bey is, although the Dean can't quite figure out "is he is or is he ain't" (62 n. 8). So it's not my purpose to defend the views of John Zerzan or George Bradford against Bookchin (although, incidentally, I'll do some of that): they are quite capable of defending themselves and I'm sure they will. Bradford, in fact, has written a lengthy rejoinder to be co-published by Autonomedia and Black & Red. But it *is* my purpose to show that in the *way* he denounces the primitivists, the Dean is, as usual, unscrupulous and malicious. When he isn't flat-out wrong he's usually irrelevant.

In rebutting a right-wing libertarian critic, I made clear two of the aspects of primitive societies (there are others) which ought to interest anarchists:

Hunter-gatherers inform our understanding and embarrass libertarians [and Bookchinists] in at least two ways. They operate the only known viable stateless societies. And they don't, except in occasional emergencies, *work* in any sense I've used the word (Black 1992: 54).

Even the Dean earlier admitted the first point: "This organic, basically preliterate or 'tribal,' society was strikingly nondomineering" (1989: 47). After all, Cultural Man is at least two million years old. He was originally a hunter-gather. He was an anatomically modern human at least 50,000 years before he adopted any other mode of subsistence. As recently as 10,000 years ago he was still only a forager (Lee & DeVore 1968c: 3). And he was still an anarchist.

Now it may well be that the life-ways of hunter-gatherers (also known as foragers) are not, as a practical matter, available for immediate adoption by disgruntled urbanites, as the Dean declaims (36). Some primitivists have said as much; John Moore, for one, is exasperated to have to keep saying so (1996: 18). Others, in my opinion, have equivocated. But that's not the point, or not the only point. A way of life is much more than a "life-style." Hunter-gatherers grow up in a habitat and learn its secrets, they have "a marvelous understanding of the habitat in which they lived; they were, after all, highly intelligent and imaginative beings" (47), Most anarchists should probably send for a lot of Loompanics books and practice up on a lot of survival skills before they even think of venturing into the wilderness on a long-term basis. Hardly any anarcho-primitivists propose to do so (to my knowledge, only one). But the point is to learn from the primitives, not necessarily to ape them.

Bob Black

Dean Bookchin, in contrast, doesn't know and doesn't want to know anything about primitives which might suggest that low-tech, non-urban anarchy is even possible — although it's the only kind of anarchy empirically proven to *be* possible. Since the whole point of the Dean's polemic is to pass judgment upon what counts as anarchism, you'd think he'd try to indict primitives as statists. As that is impossible, he changes the subject.

Repeatedly, the Dean throws what he apparently considers roundhouse punches at primitivist myths, but he never connects, either because they are not tenets of primitivism or else because they are not myths.

For instance, the Dean argues at length that hunter- gatherers have been known to modify, and not merely adapt to, their habitats, notably by the use of fire (42–43). Anthropologists, and not only the ones the Dean cites, have known that for a long time. The Australian aborigines, the quintessential foragers, set fires for various purposes which transformed their landscape, usually to their advantage (Blainey 1976: ch. 5 ["A Burning Continent"]). Shifting cultivators, such as most of the Indians of eastern North America, also fired the brush with important ecological consequences, as even historians know (Morgan 1975: ch. 3). If any primitivist ever claimed otherwise, he is wrong, but the Dean does not cite when and where he did. John Zerzan, "the anticivilizational primitivist par excellence" (39), observes, without apparent disapproval, that humans have been using fire for almost two million years (1994: 22).

To take an ecological perspective means to hypothesize general interaction among all species and between each and all species and the inanimate environment. It implies dethroning humans as the lords of nature appointed by a Judeo-Christian divinity, certainly, but it doesn't imply or presuppose that there was ever a time or a condition of society in which humans never acted upon the rest of nature but were only acted upon. Not even amoebas are that passive and quiescent (Bookchin 1989: 200).

Amazingly, Bookchin explicitly embraces the Hobbesian myth that the lives of primitive, pre-political people were nasty, brutish and short (46). For him as for Hobbes (Black 1986: 24), the purpose of the myth is to further a statist agenda.

"Our early ancestors," he remarks with satisfaction, "were more likely scavengers than hunter-gatherers" (46). How disgusting! They ate animals which were already dead! Just as we do when we shop the meat section of a supermarket. (Perhaps there are no meat sections in Burlington supermarkets. Perhaps there are no supermarkets there, just food co-ops. Why do I find it hard to summon up an image of Bookchin putting in his four hours a month bagging groceries?) Bookchin probably picked up this tidbit from Zerzan (1994: 19). Regardless, our still-prehistoric, still-anarchic ancestors must have formed other tastes in food in becoming big game hunters (42).

And these our animalistic ancestors were unhealthy too, claims the Dean. The Neanderthals suffered high rates of degenerative bone disease and serious injury (46). There is considerable controversy whether the Neanderthals *were* among our ancestors. If your ancestors are from Europe or the Levant, possibly; otherwise, almost certainly not. Admittedly, our early ancestors were more likely to be eaten by leopards and hyenas than we are (46), but for contemporary foragers, predation is a minor cause of death (Dunn 1968: 224–225). On the other hand, our leading killers, cancer and heart disease, appear infrequently among them (*ibid.:* 224), and our thousands of occupational diseases never do. Hunter-gatherers have never been afflicted by asbestosis, black lung disease, Gulf War syndrome (as I write these words, the Pentagon is finally admitting there might be such a thing) or carpal tunnel syndrome. Band societies have very low population densities, and "viral and bacterial infections cannot generally persist among small human populations" (Knauft 1987: 98). Paleolithic foragers might suffer serious or fatal injuries, but one million of them were not killed by motor vehicles in just a hundred years.

According to the Dean, prehistoric mortality statistics are "appalling": "about half died in childhood or before the age of twenty, and few lived beyond their fiftieth year" (46). Even taking these claims to be true, the aggregate figures, their vagueness aside, are highly misleading. Foraging peoples usually have a lot greater sensitivity to the carrying capacities of their habitats than techno-urbanites do. The ones who didn't have paid the price. The ones who did, and do, adjust their populations by the means at their disposal. Delayed marriage, abortion, prolonged lactation, sexual tabus, even genital surgery are among the cultural practices by which foragers hold down their birthrates (Yengoyan 1968:1941). Low-tech does have its limitations. The condom, the diaphragm, the IUD and the Pill have not been available to hunter-gatherers. Foragers have often resorted to post-partum population control as well: in other words, to infanticide and senilicide (Dunn 1968: 225).

Especially infanticide (although I suspect the Dean feels a lot more threatened by senilicide). Infanticide was probably prevalent among Pleistocene hunter-gatherers (Birdsell 1968: 236), so it's ridiculous to calculate an "average" lifespan in which the few minutes or hours some neonates were allowed to live count for as much as all the years lived by those who actually go on to *have* lives. It's as if in measuring the present-day American lifespan we included in the numerator, as 0, every conception averted by contraception and every aborted fetus, while adding each of them, scored as 1, to the denominator counting the entire population. We'd come up with a startlingly low "average" lifespan for the contemporary United States — 10 years? 20 years? — which would be utterly meaningless. When contraceptive devices became available to Nunamiut Eskimo women in 1964, there was "massive adoption" of them (Binford & Chasko 1976: 77). At this point somebody might rise up in righteous indignation — from the right, from the left, a trifling distinction — to denounce my equation of contraception, abortion and infanticide. I'm not even slightly interested in whether, or where, the Pope or any other dope draws *moral* lines among these time-honored practices. I don't equate them morally because I'm not moralizing. I equate them only with respect to the issue, the demographic issue, at hand.

Gimmickry aside, the evidence suggests that foragers live relatively long lives. The Dean's claim that the average lifespan of the !Kung San is 30 years (45) is unreferenced and misleading, Lee's censuses showed

...a substantial proportion of people over the age of 60. This high proportion (8.7 to 10.7 percent) by Third World standards contradicts the widely held notion that life in hunting and gathering societies is "nasty, brutish, and short." The argument has been made that life in these societies is so hard that people die at an early age. The Dobe area [of Botswana], by contrast, had dozens of active older persons in the population (Lee 1979: 44).

The population structure "looks like that of a developed country, for example, like that of the United States around 1900" (*ibid.;* 47). This is how two other anthropologists summarize the !Kung situation:

Although individuals who have reached maturity can expect to live into their middle 50s, life expectancy at birth is approximately 32 years, determined mainly by high infant mortality — between 10 and 20% in the first year, almost all due to infectious disease. In the traditional situation, infanticide made a small additional contribution to mortality (Konner & Shostack 1987: 12).

It is true that foragers have always lacked the technology to perpetuate the agony of their incapacitated elders as our insurance-driven system arranges for some of ours. When I visit my father in the nursing home — a stroke victim, a mentally confused cripple usually complaining of pain, 85 years old — I find it hard to consider longevity an absolute value. According to the *Iliad,* neither did Achilles:

For my mother Thetis, the goddess of the silver feet tells me I carry two sorts of destiny towards the day of my death. Either if I stay here and fight beside the city of the Trojans my return home is gone, but my glory shall be everlasting; or if I return to the beloved land of my fathers, the excellence of my glory is gone, but there will be a long life (quoted in Feyerabend 1987: 138).

For an urbanist (if less than urbane) crusader like the Dean, the relevant comparisons should be different. Primitivists like Zerzan and Bradford compare the robust lives of Paleolithic foragers with the stunted lives of those caught up in the urban/agricultural complex: "The increasingly sophisticated interpretation of the archaeological record suggests that the transition to the Neolithic was accompanied by a fairly general decline in dietary quality, evidenced in stature and decreased longevity" (Ross 1987: 12). And also a related decline in health. Almost all archeological studies "conclude that infection was a more serious problem for farmers than for their hunting and gathering forebears, and most suggest that this resulted from increased sedentism, larger population aggregates, and/or the well-established synergism between infection and malnutrition" (Cohen 1987: 269– 270). For one thing, work — and when we arrive at agriculture we arrive, unambiguously, at work — is hazardous to your health.

The fact that these are the findings of *archeological* studies of prehistoric societies renders irrelevant, for present purposes, the recent argument that the much-studied San are really just an impoverished underclass within capitalism (Wilmsen 1989). This is a controversial claim (Peters 1990) — vigorously rebutted by Richard B. Lee and like-minded anthropologists (Solway & Lee 1990) — which, predictably, Bookchin whoops up with uncritical abandon (44–45). But by definition, *pre*historic peoples cannot have been marginal to, or relics of, or devolved from historical societies. What did they devolve from? Atlantis? Lemuria? Mu? Are they the love-children of extraterrestrials ("Earth girls are easy") who, having had their exotic fun, revved up the Chariots of the Gods and rocketed off to the next off-planet pick-up scene? The artist Goya, as quoted by the Dean, once said that "the sleep of reason begets monsters" (28). Does Bookchin think that the sleeping-around of monsters begets reasonables?

And when we progress from mere agriculture to urbanism — one thing leads to another — health deteriorates even more dramatically. Throughout history, pre-industrial urban populations have usually reproduced at less than replacement levels: "Ancient cities were like tar pits, drawing country folk into their alluring but disease-ridden precincts" (Boyd & Richerson 1993: 127). The Dean is fond of the slogan that "city air makes you free" (1974: 1), but there is considerably more truth to saying that city air makes you sick (*ibid.:* 66). Urban "internal nonviability" has three sources: (1) high population density "facilitates the genesis and communication of infectious diseases"; (2) such cities "have almost invariably had poor

sanitation and hygiene, particularly with respect to water and sewage";
and (3) urbanites depend on outside sources of food, on monocultural
food production subject to crop failures and difficulties of
transportation, storage and distribution (Knauft 1987: 98).

Industrial cities have only imperfectly coped with these unhealthy
influences. They are more overcrowded than ever, with, the Dean has
shown, adverse health consequences (Herber 1965). "Urban air is
seriously polluted and urban wastes are reaching unmanageable
proportions" — furthermore:

Nothing more visibly reveals the overall decay of the modern city than
the ubiquitous filth and garbage that gathers in its streets, the noise
and massive congestion that fills its thoroughfares, the apathy of its
population toward civic issues, and the ghastly indifference of the
individual toward the physical violence that is publicly inflicted on
other members of the community (Bookchin 1974:66,67).

Even the most conspicuous health accomplishment of industrialism,
the control of disease by antibiotics, is being rolled back, as resistant
strains of disease vectors evolve. Even the food situation is
unsatisfactory, if not for precisely the traditional reasons. Most
American urbanites have unhealthy diets, and more than a few are
malnourished.

The Dean mostly obsesses about details — why not oblige him? —
such as whether contemporary hunter-gatherer societies are "pristine"
and whether hunter-gatherers have invariably been the benign
stewards of their habitats. Although these propositions are largely
irrelevant to the species "primitivism" and entirely irrelevant to its
supposed genus, "lifestyle anarchism," the ways the Dean deploys
them are relevant to his ulterior aims and exemplary of his unsavory
methods.

By "pristine" (44, 45) the Dean seems to mean the supposition that all
contemporary hunter-gatherers are living fossils who have always
lived the way they do now. As usual, when the Dean puts a loaded
word in quotation marks it's a dead giveaway that he's *not* quoting
anybody, just talking to his favorite person, himself. (Just as his

mockery of primitive "reverence for life" (42) might have been amusing — a Bookchin first — if he could only have pinned on the anarcho-primitivists a phrase employed, not by them, but by that celebrated racist paternalist, the late B'wana, Dr. Albert Schweitzer.) He might have learned that — he probably did — from John Zerzan: "surviving hunter-gatherers, who have somehow managed to evade civilization's tremendous pressures to turn them into slaves (*i.e.* farmers, political subjects, wage laborers), have all been influenced by contact with outside peoples" (1994: 29–30). The call for papers for the 1966 "Man the Hunter" conference — which the Dean blames for romanticizing foragers (37) — stated "that there is no assumption that living hunter-gatherers are somehow living relics of the Pleistocene" (quoted in Binford 1968: 274). Bookchin is beating a dead horse or, better yet, an extinct *eohippus:* "It is widely recognized that modern hunters are not pristine living relics of the Pleistocene" (Hawkes 1987: 350).

The Dean cites with some satisfaction a fairly recent article by William M. Denevan, "The Pristine Myth: The Landscape of the Americas in 1492" (1992), but for several reasons, I doubt the Dean has even read it. In the first place, the Dean only adverts to it as "cited in William K. Stevens, 'An Eden in Ancient America? Not Really,' *The New York Times* (March 30, 1993, p. CI" (63 n. 22). The newspaper story may well have been how the Dean got wind of the article — nothing wrong with that, I often follow up on tips that way — but having served that purpose, there's no reason to refer to a newspaper story which, at best, must have oversimplified the article. Second, the Dean misquotes the name of the journal. And finally, the title of the newspaper story, suggesting a debunking of the myth of "an Eden in ancient America," has absolutely nothing to do with what Denevan was really writing about, although it has everything to do with the Dean's anti-primitivist ideological agenda.

Denevan's argument, which relates only to the Western Hemisphere, is that when Europeans arrived in the New World, and for some time afterwards, the landscape they encountered — Denevan is a cultural geographer — was not "pristine" if this means it had been barely affected by tens of thousands of years of indigenous human presence.

Indian hunting, horticulture, and especially the use of fire had wrought important transformations in many stretches of the landscape. Many North American grasslands, for instance, were produced by human action, and to a lesser extent, so were the park-like woodlands of eastern North America (Morgan 1975: ch. 3; Salisbury 1982: ch. 1). But by the time the Euro-Americans moved west on a large scale, the once-numerous Indians had been decimated and much of the landscape had reverted to a tangled, pre-humanized "wilderness" the settlers mistook for pristine conditions. Denevan plausibly argues for this conclusion but does not, as the Dean does, consider it cause for celebration.

But what does this have to do with anything? A humanized landscape is not necessarily a ravaged, depleted, denaturalized landscape because there *was* a time when humans were natural.

The Dean, Professor of Social Ecology, also supposes he is saying something important when he avers that primitives may have contributed to the extinction of some species of the animals they hunted and that they may have sometimes degraded their environments (42–43). As the allegations are independent, let us address each count of the indictment separately.

Even the Dean admits that the best-known claim for induced extinction, so-called Pleistocene overkill, is "hotly debated" (63 n. 23). Rapid climatic change was indisputably part of the cause, and possibly a sufficient cause, for the extinction of overspecialized species like the mastodon. But supposing that prehistoric hunters were responsible for some extinctions — so what? Extinction has so far been the fate of almost every species to appear on this planet, and may in time be the fate of all of them. The continuation of natural life does not depend upon the continuation of any particular species, including ours. What difference does it make?

Anyway, to say that some prehistoric primitives could and did kill game animals on a large scale (42, 62–63 n. 20), as all anthropologists are well aware, does not entail that these primitives brought about the extinction of their prey. Well into historic times, the Plains Indians killed many buffalo and the Northwest Coast Indians netted many salmon without coming close to extinguishing either species. The yield, though enormous, was sustainable. It required the intrusion of industrial society to pose a real risk of extinction with its high-tech, mass-production life destruction.

An article which the Dean cites (Legge & Rowley-Conwy 1987), but must not have read very carefully — even if we disregard his mistake as to one co-author's name (62–63 n. 20 ["Rowly"]) — actually tells against his indictment of the foragers. Bookchin cites it for the conclusion "that migrating animals could have been slaughtered with devastating effectiveness by the use of corrals" (63 n. 20). Granting that — a point of no present importance — the article tells a more interesting story. The authors, archaeologists, are reporting on a site they excavated in Syria. It was first occupied by hunter-gatherers in approximately 9000 B.C. and remained occupied, with one break, well into the Neolithic (agricultural) period. The authors emphasize that this was a year-round community, not a seasonal campsite. For about a thousand years after the villagers domesticated plants, hunting — mainly gazelle hunting — continued to supply them with animal protein. By then, the authors believe, the farmers had hunted the gazelles into extinction, and only then did they take up animal husbandry to replace the meat formerly supplied by wild game.

There are two points of interest here, and each is adverse to the Dean. Hunter-gatherers were *not* responsible for the extinction of the gazelles: their agricultural descendants were. These villagers had long since ceased to be foragers by the time they finished off the gazelles (locally, that is: the animals survived elsewhere). More important, they'd never really *been* hunter-gatherers in the sense in which hunter-gatherers interest primitivists and ought to interest all anarchists.

Anthropologists have recently resolved an ambiguity in the expression "hunter-gatherers" (cf. Murdock 1968: 13–15). It refers to two kinds of society, not one: nonsedentary and sedentary. What they have in common is that they hunt and/or gather rather than plant/and or herd. They do not domesticate either plants or animals (in a few such societies, dogs are domesticated, but not as a food source). What separates them is whether they occupy locations on a long-term or short-term basis. The occupants of the Syrian site were always "hunters" in the obvious respect that, like many members of the National Rifle Association, they hunted animals. But they more closely resembled such Northwest Coast Indians as the Kwakiutl in that they were the permanent, year-round occupants of favored, restricted locations which afforded them sustenance. They were not the same sort of "hunter-gatherers" as the Australian aborigines, the San/Bushmen, the Pygmies, the Great Basin Shoshone and many others for whom frequent relocation was the condition of successful adaptation to their habitats. Sedentary hunter-gatherers are socially much more like sedentary agriculturalists and urbanites than they are like foragers who are routinely on the move. Their societies exhibit class stratification, hereditary chiefs, sometimes even slavery (Kelly 1991; Renouf 1991: 90–91, 98, 101 n. 1; cf. Renouf 1989 for a prehistoric European example). It is from these societies that the city and the state emerged — together.

Possibly more relevant is the claim that primitives are not necessarily "ecologically benign" (42), and there's no reason to suppose they always are. As Denevan says, sometimes "Indians lived in harmony with nature with sustainable systems of resource management" and sometimes they didn't (1992: 370). But Devevan was not generalizing about primitives, he was generalizing about Indians. He nowhere adduces a single example of Amerindian hunter-gatherers who degraded their environment, and neither does Bookchin, although I wouldn't lose a lot of sleep if it turned out that there was one, or even more than one group like that. A small-scale society which fouled its own nest would probably not survive, but the environmental damage it did would be localized. A small-scale society which by some combination of insight and accident settled into a sustainable relationship with its ecosystem would be much more likely to persist. Existing foraging societies may not all have been around for millennia, but they've endured at least for centuries.

"Primitivism" is not "indigenism," *i.e.,* pan-Indian racial nationalism with a left-wing spin such as Ward Churchill serves up. "Primitive" and "Indian" are not synonyms. Most primitives were never Indians and many pre-Columbian Indians weren't primitives. The Dean reports that "forest overclearing and the failure of subsistence agriculture undermined Mayan society and contributed to its collapse" (43). One only has to refer to his own footnote to identify his references (64 n. 25) from "The Collapse of Classic Maya Civilization" in *The Collapse of Ancient States and Civilizations* to *The Collapse of Complex Societies* in order to notice that he's not referring to foragers or primitives, he's referring to a *civilization,* the state-organized, urban-based, agricultural, priest-ridden, class-stratified Mayan civilization. Civilizations have a long history of occasioning environmental destruction whether the civilized be red, white, black or yellow: they have belonged to all of these races. Is this news to Professor Social Ecology?

Probably the most amusing aspect of the Dean's campaign against the primitivists is how blatantly self-contradictory it is (Jarach 1996). While he wants to represent primitive life-ways as undesirable, the decisive point is that they are, for us, simply impossible: "Anyone who advises us to significantly, even drastically, reduce our technology is also advising us, in all logic, to go back to the 'stone age' — at least to the Neolithic or Paleolithic (early, middle, or late)" (36).

To digress for just a bit, consider how idiotic this assertion is. The Dean says that any significant rollback of technology would reduce us to, at best, the Neolithic, the New Stone Age. But obviously there was a lot of technological progress, if that's what it was, between the Neolithic Revolution (agriculture) which commenced a few thousand years ago and the Megamachine which dominates us now. The Dean's beloved Athenian *polis,* for instance, exploited a technology much inferior to what we moderns command but far beyond what the Neolithic farmers, the earliest farmers, had to work with. Early medieval Europe, an almost entirely rural society, quickly developed new technology (such as the mould-board plough) beyond anything that urban-oriented Greco-Roman civilization ever did.

John Zerzan's unspeakable heresy, as the Dean sees it, is that Zerzan thinks that prehistoric hunter-gatherers did not just fail to "innovate technological change" (38), they *refused* domestication and the division of labor. For the Dean, progress is an offer you can't refuse. But then, sublimely oblivious to the inconsistency, he goes on to say that some primitive societies *have,* in his value-laden word, "devolved" from more complex societies (44). The Mayans devolved from civilization (43). The Yuqui foragers of the Bolivian forest devolved from "a slave-holding pre-Columbian society" which was horticultural (45). Even the San have "literally devolved — probably very much against their desires — from horticultural social systems" (44; cf. Wilmsen 1989).

We may "never have any way of knowing whether the lifeways of today's foraging cultures accurately mirror those of our ancestral past" (43) — actually, archeology and paleoecology have come up with some ways — but we have an easy way to find out if the San would rather be gardeners than foragers. We can ask them. This would never occur to the Dean, for whom contemporary foragers are little more than talking dogs, but it occurred to Richard B. Lee when he lived with and studied the San in the '60s: "when a Bushman was asked why he hadn't taken to agriculture he replied: 'Why should we plant, when there are so many mongongo nuts in the world?'" (Lee 1968: 33).

There are many examples of *voluntary* "devolution." The ancestors of most Plains Indian tribes were agriculturalists. There is absolutely no reason to suppose they were forced off their farmlands and onto the plains by environmental pressures or aggression from other tribes. When the horse, introduced by the Spanish, found its way north, these Indians seized upon this new technology to "devolve" from sedentary agriculture to nomadic buffalo hunting. We'll never know for sure why they made this choice. Was buffalo meat tastier than corn? Was hunting more fun than farming? Was a frequent change of scenery more interesting than being stuck forever in Mudville-on-the-Missouri? Whatever it was, it *was* a choice. Maybe we have a choice too.

Bob Black

Chapter 8: In Search of the Primitivists Part II: Primitive Affluence

According to the Dean, the notion of primitive affluence is some silliness the hippies smoked up and put over on the anthropologists in the '60s:

Much of [George Bradford's] "critical anthropology" appears to derive from ideas propounded at the "Man the Hunter" symposium, convened in April 1966 at the University of Chicago. Although most of the papers contributed to this symposium were immensely valuable, a number of them conformed to the naive mystification of "primitivity" that was percolating through the 1960s counter-culture — and that lingers on to this day. The hippie culture, which influenced quite a few anthropologists of the time, averred that hunting-gathering peoples today had been bypassed by the social and economic forces at work in the rest of the world and still lived in a pristine state, as isolated remnants of Neolithic and Paleolithic lifeways. Further, as hunter-gatherers, their lives were notably healthy and peaceful, living then as now on an ample natural largess (37).

The chief villain of the piece was anthropologist Richard B. Lee, who had "estimated that the caloric intake of 'primitive' peoples was quite high and their food supply abundant, making for a kind of virginal 'affluence' in which people needed to forage only a few hours each day" (37–38).

In the above-quoted passage, "it would take a full-sized essay in itself to unscramble, let alone refute, this absurd balderdash, in which a few truths are either mixed with or coated in sheer fantasy" (37). The Dean refers to a passage he quotes from Bradford, but might have been referring to his favorite subject — himself — except that there aren't even a few truths in *his* passage, not even mixed or coated with fantasy.

The revision of the Hobbesian postulate that primitive life is nasty, brutish and short commenced, not at the "Man the Hunter" symposium in 1966 (Lee & DeVore 1968), but at the symposium on band societies in Ottawa in 1965 (Damas 1969). The Chicago symposium only extended the theses of the pioneering Ottawa gathering (Renouf 1991: 89–90). April 1965 and even April 1966 (Lee & DeVore 1968: vii) are implausibly early dates to assume much hippie influence on academic scholarship, and the Dean adduces no evidence in support of his self-serving conjecture. There's no trace of counterculture influence, for instance, in Bookchin's 1965 book *Crisis in Our Cities* (Herber 1965) or his 1965 essay "Ecology and Revolutionary Thought" (Bookchin 1971: 55- 82). Indeed, back when his memories were more recent and his memory perhaps better, Bookchin wrote that "the hippie movement was just getting underway in New York when 'Ecology and Revolutionary Thought' was published" (*ibid.: 29).* In contrast, the hippie movement bulks large in his 1970 essay opportunistically lauding youth culture (Bookchin 1970: 51–63). The times they were a-changin'. To Bookchin's annoyance, they still are.

If there is any relationship between '60s hippie culture and the anti-Hobbesian turn in anthropology, it is of the sort the statisticians call a spurious relationship. That is, the variables are associated with each other, not as cause and effect, but as consequences of a common cause (Babbie 1992: 416). The common cause would have been the general climate of distrust of authority and orthodoxy.

If you read the Dean's passage with more care than it was written with, it's noticeable that he attributes most of the malign influence on the primitivists, not to the anthropologists, but to the hippies. I am drawing on my own distant memories here, but my recollection is that what the hippies romanticized was *tribal* society on the model, usually ill-understood, of certain pacific Native American tribes like the Hopi and the Navajo. At the time, Bookchin apparently thought so too. "In its demands for tribalism," among others, "the Youth Culture prefigures, however inchoately, a joyous communist and classless society" (Bookchin 1970: 59). Unless they were attending graduate school, few hippies would have been acquainted with what Bookchin calls the "'Man the Hunter' timewarp" (39), which was expressly and only about revising the Hobbesian view of *hunter-gatherers.*

Bob Black

For the most part, hunter-gatherers don't even *live* in tribes, they live in bands (Lee & DeVore 1968b: 7–8). In contrast, tribal peoples — horticulturalists or herders — occupy a social space "between bands and states" (Gregg 1991). Many of their societies are also anarchist and as such are also interesting, as well as interesting in their own right, but necessarily there are not as many valid generalizations about primitives as there are about foragers. All foragers are primitives, but not all primitives are foragers.

In a way, it's Bradford's fault for inviting the Dean to foment confusion. If the Dean quotes him correctly — always a big *if* where the Dean is concerned — Bradford wrote in 1991 that the "official" anthropological view of foragers is the Hobbesian one. That was already changing even when Marshall Sahlins made the same point in his 1968 essay "The Original Affluent Society" (Sahlins 1971: ch. 1). Today the "current model" (Renouf 1991: 89–90) is the one advanced at the Ottawa and Chicago conferences: "although the more idealized aspects of the Lee and DeVore model are commonly acknowledged, I think it is fair to say that no fundamental revision of it has been made" (*ibid.:* 90). Similarly, another anthropologist refers to the continuing prevalence of "the revised general version of hunter-gatherers of the mid- 1960s" (Conkey 1984: 257). John Zerzan, not George Bradford, is correct in saying that "a nearly complete reversal in anthropological orthodoxy has come about, with important implications" (1994: 16). Bradford's failure to update the opinions he's expressed since the 1970s — which is typical of the *Fifth Estate* — afforded the Dean an undeserved opportunity to claim scientific respectability for a viewpoint long since discredited.

Bradford's other mistake, eagerly exploited by the Dean, is that he allegedly wrote that the revisionist view is based on "greater access to the views of primal people and their native descendants" (37). That gave the Dean his chance to dismiss primitive affluence as the "edenic" myth of nostalgic natives (36) feeding their fantasies, and perhaps their peyote, to credulous white hippies.

This is all wrong. It was the *earliest* studies of hunter-gatherers, including classic accounts by Kroeber, Boas and Radcliffe-Brown, which relied on older informants' memories of conditions 25–50 years before, on "ethnographic reconstructions of situations which were no longer intact" (Lee & DeVore 1968c: 5–6). The Man the Hunter symposium, far from overlooking this method's shortcomings, made that a "central theme" (*ibid.:* 6). Contemporary anthropologists have *lesser,* not greater access to the views of so-called primal people. In the first place, primal people are disappearing almost as rapidly as leftists are. And secondly, Western anthropologists no longer enjoy as much "access" as they did when the people they studied were subject to Western colonial rule. Most indigenous peoples now have more power to determine whether and on what terms they will receive resident and even visiting ethnographers. Some exclude them entirely. And the national governments of some former colonial possessions which are now independent states restrict or exclude foreign anthropologists for a variety of reasons (Beals 1969: 20–27).

More important, the affluence thesis is based on observation and measurement, not myth and memory. Richard B. Lee concluded that the !Kung San/Bushmen did remarkably little work compared to us — not by sitting at the feet of the Old Wise Man like they do at Goddard College — but by following the San around to see what they were doing and for how long. He based his conclusions as to the sufficiency of their diet on measuring the calories they ingested and expended (Lee 1969, 1979), something rarely done previously. One of the resulting articles was titled "!Kung Bushmen Subsistence: An Input-Output Analysis" (Lee 1969). This is science at its most muscular, not free-form fantasy.

It doesn't necessarily follow, of course, that if San society is in a very tangible, measurable sense leisurely and affluent, then so are all or most other foraging societies. But on the Hobbesian new, the San as they lived in the 1960s were impossible, so the Hobbesian view in the muscular form espoused by the Dean has to be qualified or, as the social scientists say, "specified" (the scope of its validity narrowed) (Babbie 1992: 421–422) or else rejected altogether. And what's so intriguing is that the San live their affluence in the arid Kalahari Desert, not someplace approximating the Garden of Eden (Zerzan 1994: 29). If foraging life could be affluent there, it might have been affluent almost everywhere — and almost everywhere is where pre-historic humans lived, as foragers, for 99% of human existence (Lee & DeVore 1968c: 5). The civilized, in contrast, find it very difficult to sustain an affluent lifestyle in the desert outside of a few special locations like Palm Springs and Kuwait (cf. Lévi-Strauss 1962: 5 [quoted in Feyerabend (1987): 112 n. 14)]).

These implications have not only reoriented fieldwork, they have also occasioned the reinterpretation of already available accounts of hunter-gatherers, both historical sources and formal ethnographies. Sahlins (1971: ch. 1) did some of both in "The Original Affluent Society," whose conclusions he'd previewed as a discussant at the Man the Hunter symposium (Lee & DeVore 1968: 85–89). The abundant historical accounts of the Australian aborigines, for all their misperceptions, if carefully read, confirm the affluence thesis. And the earlier ethnographers of hunter-gatherers, although they had often announced as their conclusions the Hobbesian party line, report ample data which contradict those conclusions. Anthropologists who once slighted written, historical sources relating to foragers such as the San are now combing them very carefully (*e.g.,* Parkington 1984).

Unlike Bradford, the Man the Hunter anthropologists were not interested in primitive animism, harmony with nature, or "ecstatic techniques," a phrase the Dean attributes to Bradford (36). Anthropologists had long since documented beyond any reasonable possibility of refutation all these aspects of many primitive cultures. What the Man-the-Hunter revisionists added was precisely what the Dean claims is missing, the social dimension: "Egalitarianism, sharing, and low work effort were stressed, as was the importance of gathering foods and, by extension, women's direct role in the economy" (Renouf 1991: 89). The Dean's entire rhetorical strategy is as misdirected as it is malicious. Primitivists contrast the orderly anarchy and the generous egalitarianism of foragers with the chaotic statism and class hierarchy of urban civilization. The Dean dredges up *one* foraging society, the Yuqui of Bolivia, which, he claims, includes the institution of hereditary slavery — although he has to admit that "this feature is now regarded as a feature of former horticultural lifeways" (45).

You could hardly ask for a better example of the exception that proves the rule. There were only 43 Yuqui at contact in the 1950s, far below the minimum — usually put at about 500 — for social viability. They are probably descended from a Guaraní raiding party of the late pre-Columbian period which was unable to find its way back to Paraguay. Remarkably, they maintained vestiges of slavery, something "difficult to imagine, but it did exist." The Dean neglects to mention that upon falling into the clutches of the missionaries, this social splinter abandoned both foraging and slavery (Stearman 1989). This example proves, at the most, that foraging societies are not always anarchist and egalitarian, leaving untouched the conclusion, which even the Dean doesn't deny, that they are *almost* always anarchist and egalitarian.

On the other hand, in thirty years of celebrating urbanism, the Dean has yet to identify a stable, anarchic, egalitarian urban society. Perhaps revolutionary Barcelona approximated one for a few months in 1936–1937, and Paris in 1968 for several weeks. But at best these are only blips on a social screen of almost unrelieved urban statism and class stratification. These "outliers," as the statisticians refer to rare values of variables, far outside the range of all others, do remind us — as do the Yuqui — of the human capacity for extreme social plasticity. As such, they hearten me, but they fail to persuade me that "some kind of urban community is not only the environment of humanity: it is its destiny" (Bookchin 1974: 2). I don't think anatomy is destiny and I don't think urbanity is destiny either.

Chapter 9: From Primitive Affluence to Labor-Enslaving Technology

One tendency which surely belongs on the Dean's enemies short list is zero-work, the critique of work as such, "the notion that the abolition of work is possible and desirable: that genuine, unconditioned needs can be met by voluntary playlike activity enjoyed for its own sake" (Black 1996d: 22). Zero-work may well be the *only* programmatic position shared by everybody the Dean targets, even L. Susan Brown (1995). The Left That Was not only posited work as a necessity, it regarded it as almost a sacrament. And while zero-work is not the same thing as such Bookchin bugbears as hedonism and primitivism, it complements them nicely. It *is* an important Bookchin target, but he attacks it with potshots, not the usual scattershot. There may be several reasons for his uncharacteristic circumspection.

In his younger days ("younger" being, of course, a relative term), Bookchin understood that dealing radically with what he called "toil" was a crucial dimension of post-scarcity anarchism: "The distinction between pleasurable work and onerous toil should always be kept in mind" (1971: 92). Even 25 years ago, the productive forces had developed "to a point where even toil, not only material scarcity, is being brought into question" (Bookchin 1970: 53). For the traditional left, the answer to the question of work was to eliminate unemployment, rationalize production, develop the productive forces, and reduce the hours of work. To this program the ultra-left, such as the council communists and the anarcho-syndicalists, added workers' control of production according to one formula or another. These reforms, even if completely successful on their own terms, fall short of any *qualitative* transformation of the experience of productive activity. Why doesn't the Dean just contradict his former opinion without admitting it, as he does with so many others?

It may be because zero-work is one dimension of avant garde anarchism which on Bookchin's terms looks *progressive* not regressive — a double irony, as heterodox anarchists tend to disbelieve in progress. Reduced hours of work is an ancient demand of the left (and of the labor movement [Hunnicutt 1988]). Marx considered it the precondition of passage from the realm of necessity to the realm of freedom (1967: 820), just like Bookchin (Clark 1984: 55). Anarchists agreed: "The eight-hour day which we officially enjoy is the cause for which the Haymarket anarchists of 1886 paid with their lives" (Black 1992: 29). Over a century ago, Kropotkin argued that it was then *already* possible to reduce the working day to four or five hours, with retirement by age 45 or 50 (1995: 96). What would his estimate be today: 40 or 50 minutes? Since the Dean believes (however erroneously) that technological progress reduces "toil," at least potentially (26), he has to believe that the abolition of work is an ever- increasingly practical possibility. He can only criticize zero-workers, not as reactionaries, but as ahead of their time. And that debunks the whole notion of lifestyle anarchism as a surrender to the prevailing climate of reaction.

The Dean might have other reasons not to be conspicuous or even explicit in his rejection of zero-work. Lifestyle anarchists have supposedly withdrawn "from the social domain that formed the principal arena of earlier anarchists" (2) because lifestyle anarchism "is concerned with a 'style' rather than a society" (34). But for an old Marxist like Bookchin, labor is the very essence of the social: "Labor, perhaps more than any single human activity, underpins contemporary relationships among people on every level of experience" (1982: 224). In the importance they attach to the labor process, zero-workers resemble traditional socialists, not "the growing 'inwardness' and narcissism of the yuppie generation" (9). Work is about *real life,* not lifestyle or hairstyle.

Finally, there might be a very personal source of the Dean's relative reticence. His usual method is to focus on one or two prominent expositors of each malign aspect of lifestyle anarchism. Were he to deal with zero-work that way he would probably have to deal with me. As the author of "The Abolition of Work" (Black 1986: 17–33), a widely read essay which has been published in seven languages, and other zero-work writings (Black 1992: ch. 1; 1996b), I would be the single most convenient whipping-boy. But Bookchin never refers to me with respect to zero-work or anything else. What am I, chopped liver?

I can only speculate why I was spared, except by implication, the Dean's wrath. The flattering suggestion has been made that he feared my polemic powers and hoped I'd ignore his diatribe unless personally provoked by it (Jarach 1996: 3). If so, he miscalculated. I'm a better friend to my friends than that, and besides, I like a good fight. I'm not the kind of guy who says: "First they came for the anarcho-liberal individualists, but I said nothing, for I was not an anarcho-liberal individualist; next they came for the mystics, but I said nothing, for I was not a mystic; next they came for the primitivists, but I said nothing, for I was not a primitivist," etc.

If anything, I am peeved to be overlooked. Bookchin's enemies list looks to be for the anarchists of the '90s what Nixon's enemies list was for the liberals of the '70s, an honor roll. I've previously flattened a nobody — his name doesn't matter — who pushed the same line as Bookchin (Black 1992: 181–193; Black & Gunderloy 1992) although that one also happened not to mention my name. For me, the political is the personal. An attack upon all is an attack upon one. Solidarity forever — or make my day! ¡No paserán — baby!

We have already seen (Chapter 9) how the Dean blithely misrepresents the best current understanding of how, and how long, foragers work — if that is even the word for what they do for a living, or rather, for the living that they do. As I've summarized the situation in my book *Friendly Fire:*

In addition to shorter hours, "flextime" and the more reliable "safety net" afforded by food sharing, foragers' work is more satisfying than most modern work. We awaken to the alarm clock; they sleep a lot, night and day. We are sedentary in our buildings in our polluted cities; they move about breathing the fresh air of the open country. We have bosses; they have companions. Our work typically implicates one, or at most a few hyper-specialized skills, if any; theirs combines handwork and brainwork in a versatile variety of activities, exactly as the great Utopians called for (Black 1992: 33).

I've cited ample supporting references in that book (which the Dean is surely familiar with, if less than happy with) as also in this one (cf. Zerzan 1994: 171–185 [Bibliography]). All Bookchin can do is fulminate that the primitive affluence thesis is hippie hokum, an *ad hominem* insult which is irrelevant as well as untrue.

The Dean is equally wrong about work — and the relationship of technology to work — in other forms of society. In *Friendly Fire* I summarized some of the evidence (there's lots more) that as technology advances, the quantity of work increases and the quality of the work experience declines (Black 1992: 19–41). In general, there's no such thing as labor-saving technology. There's usually, at best, only labor- rearranging technology, which from the worker's perspective is sort of like "emigrating from Romania to Ethiopia in search of a better life" (*ibid.:* 13). Capitalists develop and deploy new technology, not to reduce labor, but to reduce the price of labor. The higher the tech, the lower the wages and the smaller the work-force.

When he descends from declamation to detail, the Dean exposes his ignorance of the real history of work and technology. The two examples he adduces are evidence enough. Here's his cartoon history of Southern agriculture:

In the South, plantation owners needed slave "hands" in great part because the machinery to plant and pick cotton did not exist; indeed, American tenant farming has disappeared over the past two generations because new machinery was introduced to replace the labor of "freed" black share-croppers (35).

In other words, Bookchin blames slavery on technological backwardness, not on a capitalist world-system which assigned to the South the function of export monoculture. But cotton was of minor importance in the low-tech colonial economy of the seventeenth and eighteenth centuries when slaves were raising other export crops such as tobacco, rice and indigo (McCusker & Menard 1985). As every schoolchild knows, technical progress *strengthened* slavery, which had been languishing, with the conjunction of the cotton gin with the textiles-based Industrial Revolution in Britain (Scheiber, Vatter & Faulkner 1976: 130–134).

If what Bookchin says about slaveholders makes sense, then*every* ruling class is off the hook. The plantation owners "needed" slaves "in great part" because they lacked machines to do their work for them. Presumably industrialists "needed" child labor for the same reason. Athenian citizens "needed" slaves because their technology was inadequate to peel their grapes, give them blowjobs, and satisfy the many other needs of a civic-minded citizenry with aims so lofty that they could not be troubled with earning their own keep. "Need" is socially and economically relative. No doubt the Southern planters and the Athenian citizens needed slaves, but did the slaves need the Southern planters or the Athenian citizens?

The Deans's other example is also maladroit. It's that classic instrument of women's liberation, the washing machine: "Modern working women with children could hardly do without washing machines to relieve them, however minimally, from their daily domestic labors — before going to work to earn what is often the greater part of their households' income" (49). In other words, the washing machine reinforces the domestic sexual division of labor *and* enables women to be proletarianized — to enter the paid labor force at the bottom (Black 1992: 29–30). Thanks to technology, modern working women get to do the unpaid drudge-work, the "shadow work" (Illich 1981) of the patriarchal household, *plus* the underpaid capitalist drudge-work of the office, the restaurant and even the factory. The washing machine, and household technology in general, never saved women any labor-time. It just raised performance standards (with a Maytag, no excuse any more if your laundry's not *brighter than white)* or else displaced effort to other tasks like child care (Cowan 1974, 1983). I doubt Bookchin does his own laundry, and not only because he's always airing his dirty linen in public.

In Bookchin's civic Utopia, "a high premium would be placed on labour-saving devices — be they computers or automatic machinery — that would free human beings from needless toil and give them unstructured leisure time for their self-cultivation as individuals and citizens" (1989: 197). To believe in that is, for someone as ignorant as Bookchin, an act of faith. In recent decades productivity, driven by high technology far beyond anything the Dean anticipated, has increased prodigiously — more than doubling since 1948 (Schor 1991: 1–2, 5, 29). Oddly enough, not even "material scarcity," much less "toil," has diminished. Real income has fallen at the same time hours of work have increased (Black 1994: 31–32; Black 1996b: 45). Even the Dean has noticed, literally on page one, "the growing impoverishment of millions of people" at the same time that "the intensity of exploitation has forced people in growing numbers to accept a work week typical of the last century" (1). What he hasn't noticed is that the paradox of more progress, more productivity, more poverty and more work calls *his* essentially Marxist celebration of the development of the productive forces, as he might say, "into question."

The Dean admits that "many technologies are inherently domineering and ecologically dangerous" (34), but he cannot imagine that they increase and worsen work. Really he just *doesn't care.* He hasn't devoted any sustained attention to work since *Post-Scarcity Anarchism* (1971). After 25 years as a college bureaucrat, the factory is a distant memory. His 1989 primer summarizing his views on remaking society devoted all of two sentences to work with but a perfunctory affirmation of rotation of tasks (1989: 195). All Bookchin cares about any more is politics and ecology, in that order. Provided a technology is neither "domineering" nor "dangerous," its impact on work means nothing to him.

Nothing better dramatizes the Dean's self-deception and irrelevance than the contrast between his fervor for politics and his indifference to work. He believes, because he wants to believe, that "seldom in recent memory has there been a more compelling popular sentiment for a new politics" (59). That contradicts his characterization of the epoch as privatistic, personalistic and apolitical. The truth is that seldom in recent memory has there been a more compelling sentiment for *no* politics.

On the other hand, work is if anything more salient, if less liked, in the lives of ordinary people than it's been in decades. Longer hours, lower real incomes, and employment insecurity have done nothing to compensate for the joyless and often humiliating experience of the work itself. In the 1960s Bookchin, ever alert to sniffing out potentially revolutionary sources of social malaise, expressed approval of the younger generation's contempt for the work trap (Bookchin 1970: 54, 61; 1971: 175–176; cf. 1994: 30). But while other Bookchin-approved tendencies, like youth culture, were recuperated, a widening revolt against work became a persistent feature of the American workplace (DeLeon 1996: 196–197; Zerzan 1988: 170–183). Spontaneous and acephalous, it could neither be bought out by bosses nor organized by leftists. The overworked and the unemployed — now *there's* a potentially revolutionary force (Black 1996a).

Chapter 10: Shut Up, Marxist!

As a matter of course, unless ideology withers away, it eventually hardens into dogma. After Jesus comes Paul, and eventually some Pope, Innocent in name only. That Bookchinism would calcify into a creed after no very long time is no surprise. Even in its prime it was arthritic with Rousseau, St.-Simon, Marx and Arendt. It was always ambiguous about technology and scarcity. Its ecological content was always at odds with its civism, to which, in retrospect, ecology seems to have always been an accessory, an add-on. It's marred by eccentricities as various as primitive gerontocracy and Swiss anarchy. It's unredeemed by irony, much less humor. What's amazing is that Bookchin isn't leaving Bookchinism to its Plekhanovs, Kautskys and Lenins. He's vulgarizing his ideology *himself.*

As the *Green Anarchist* reviewer observes, the Dean now "goes on to crudely reduce or reject all that's best in his *Ecology of Freedom,"* forsaking dialectics for dualism (Anonymous 1996: 22). In fact he's gone back on the best of everything he's written. This latest tract by the author of "Listen, Marxist!" might have been titled "Listen to the Marxist!" The author of "Desire and Need" (2) denounces desire as greed. The benign, "conciliatory" animism of organic society (Bookchin 1982: 98) has become "an inexplicable, often frightening dream world that they [the ignorant jungle bunnies] took for reality" (42). The author who acclaimed the drop-out culture (Bookchin 1970: 63 n. 1) now vilifies "lumpen lifeways" (56). The author who cannot spit out the word "zine" without contemptuous quotation marks (51) used to publish a zine, *Comment,* himself (Bookchin 1979: 28). There must be hundreds of these contradictions. The Dean is oblivious to all of them.

"Certainly," decrees the Dean, "it is already no longer possible, in my view, to call oneself an anarchist without adding a qualifying adjective to distinguish oneself from lifestyle anarchists" (61). That's the most reasonable proposal in the entire essay. I suggest he call himself a "Bookchinist anarchist" or, if his overweening modesty forbids, an "anti-lifestyle anarchist." Nobody will know what he's talking about, so introducing himself that way might stimulate curiosity about his views, much as would introducing oneself as a Two-Seed-in-the-Spirit Primitive Baptist.

Fated to failure, however, is any attempt to standardize the terminology on Bookchin's tendentious terms. Most anarchists would already rather answer to "social anarchist" than "lifestyle anarchist." Reading the Dean's tract won't turn any lifestyle anarchists — who number in the "thousands" (1) — into social anarchists, but it might encourage them to adopt protective coloration (red). We will all be social anarchists, even if, like Bookchin, we aren't anarchists at all. Bookchinists might retaliate by calling themselves "*very* social anarchists," but you see where that would lead. They need a name nobody else wants. How about "Marxist"?

Chapter 11: Anarchy after Leftism

In one respect, Murray Bookchin is right in almost the only way he's still capable of, *i.e.,* for the wrong reasons. The anarchists *are* at a turning point. For the first time in history, they are the *only* revolutionary current. To be sure, not all anarchists are revolutionaries, but it is no longer possible to be a revolutionary without being an anarchist, in fact if not in name.

Throughout its existence as a conscious current, anarchism has been shadowed and usually overshadowed by leftism in general, and Marxism in particular. Especially since the formation of the Soviet Union, anarchism has effectively (and therefore ineffectively) defined itself with reference to Marxism. The reduction of anarchists to satellites of the Communists, especially in revolutionary situations, is so regular a feature of their modern history that it can't be an accident. Fixated on their great rival, the anarchists have *competed* with Marxists on their own leftist terms and so the anarchists have always lost.

Bob Black

Marxism was already ideologically bankrupt by the time European Communism collapsed. As ideology, Marxism is now merely a campus — and mostly a faculty — phenomenon, and even as such its persistence is mostly parasitic upon feminism and the racial nationalisms. As a state system, what remains of Marxism is merely Oriental despotism, unthinkable as a model for the West. Suddenly, seventy years of anarchist excuses became irrelevant.

Although these developments caught the anarchists, like everybody else, by surprise, they were not as unprepared as they would have been twenty years earlier. Many of them had, if not by design, then by drift and default, strayed from their traditional position as "the 'left wing' of 'all socialisms'" (6) — but not by moving to the right. Like many other North Americans, they were unable to discern any difference between left and right of such importance that they felt compelled to declare for one or the other. As the leftist veneer — or tarnish — they typically acquired in college wore off, an indigenous anti-authoritarianism showed through. The Marxists they encountered on campus were too ridiculous to be taken seriously as rivals or reference points. (That some of them were professors made them that much more ridiculous.) More than ever before, some anarchists insisted on a "personalistic" grounding of politics in the experience of everyday life, and they correspondingly opened up to theorists like the situationists for whom the critique of everyday life was a first principle. They took to dumpster-diving among the discards of doctrines and cultures to fashion, like a collage, recombinant world-pictures of their own. And if Nietzsche's definition is right — that man is the animal who laughs — then they recovered some of their humanity too.

Now I admit this picture is too rosy because it's not red enough. A fraction of North American anarchists, mostly syndicalists, remain out-and-out leftists. As such, they share the decline of the rest of the left. They no longer include any first-rate or even second-rate thinkers. Other pockets of anarchists act as auxiliaries of sub-leftist, particularist ideologies like feminism and Third World nationalism (including indigenism) — the larger hunks of wreckage from the New Left. These too have produced their logorrheics but nobody with anything to say. Many other anarchists retain vestiges of leftism (not always a bad thing). What's important is how many of them, whatever their lingering influences, simply aren't leftists any more. The Dean's jeremiad expresses his shock of recognition at this unprecedented state of affairs.

The precondition for any substantial increase in anarchist influence is for anarchists to make explicit and emphatic their break with the left. This does *not* mean placing the critique of the left at the center of analysis and agitation. On the contrary, that's always been a symptom of anarchism's satellite status. It is enough to identify leftism, as the occasion arises, as all it really is, a variant of hegemonic ideology — a loyal opposition — which was formerly effective in recuperating revolutionary tendencies. There's no reason for anarchists to inherit an accursed share of the left's unpopularity. Let's make our *own* enemies.

And our own friends. Since there really is something anarchist about some popular tendencies, we should try to make some anarchist tendencies popular. Certain anarchist themes both old and new resonate with certain widespread attitudes. It isn't necessarily elitist or manipulative to circulate the proposition that anarchism explicates and elaborates various inchoate anti-authoritarian tendencies. This can be done in an imperialistic and opportunistic fashion, but I believe it can also be done, judiciously, in good faith. If we're mistaken, no harm done, we just won't go over very well, something we're used to. Many people will surely shrink, at least initially, from drawing the anarchist conclusions we suggest their own attitudes and values tend toward. Then again, some others may not, not even initially — especially the young.

Besides, making converts is not the only purpose of anarchist agitprop. It may also enlarge the chokingly constricted range of North American political discourse. We may never bring most of the intelligentsia over, but we can soften them up. We can reduce some of them to sympathizers, to what the Stalinists called fellow travellers, to what Lenin called useful idiots. They will traduce our ideas but also, in some mutilated form, send them around and legitimate them in the sense that they are to be taken seriously. And in so doing they will weaken their own power to counter them if and when these ideas are taken seriously enough to be acted upon by those who understand them.

Americans (and undoubtedly others, but I'll stick with the American context Bookchin addresses) really are in a certain sense "anarchistic." I'm not going to pretend, like David De Leon (1978), that there is something innately and immemorially anarchist about Americans. Our beliefs and behavior have long been otherwise in important respects. Most contemporary American anarchists and other radicals — and I include myself here — have been consciously and conspicuously anti-American. In college, I majored in history, but I took courses only in European history, because Europeans had a revolutionary heritage which we Americans (I assumed) did not. Much later I learned that Americans have at times been much more revolutionary (and so, to me, more interesting) than I originally supposed. While this discovery didn't transform me into a patriot, as my anti-Gulf War activities demonstrate (Black 1992: ch. 9), it did kindle a sympathetic interest in American history which I am still pursuing. Anarchy is at once very much an elaboration of certain American values and at the same time antithetical to certain others. So it makes no sense for American anarchists to be pro-American *or* anti-American. They should be themselves — their one indisputable area of expertise — and see what that leads to.

Post-leftist anarchy is positioned to articulate — not a program — but a number of revolutionary themes with contemporary relevance and resonance. It is, unlike Bookchinism, unambiguously anti-political, and many people are anti-political. It is, unlike Bookchinism, hedonistic, and many people fail to see why life is not to be lived enjoyably if it is to be lived at all. It is, unlike Bookchinism, "individualistic" in the sense that if the freedom and happiness of the individual — *i.e.,* each and every really existing person, every Tom, Dick and Murray — is not the measure of the good society, what is? Many people wonder what's wrong with wanting to be happy. Post-leftist anarchy is, unlike Bookchinism, if not necessarily rejective, then at least suspicious of the chronically unfulfilled liberatory promise of high technology. And maybe most important of all is the massive revulsion against work, an institution which has become less and less important to Bookchin at the same time it's become more and more important, and oppressive, to people outside academia who actually have to work. Most people would rather do less work than attend more meetings. Which is to say, most people are smarter, and saner, than Murray Bookchin is. Post-leftist anarchists mostly don't regard our times one-dimensionally, as either a "decadent, bourgeoisified era" (1) of "social reaction" (9) *or* as the dawning of the Age of Aquarius. They tend toward pessimism, but not usually as much as the Dean does. The system, unstable as ever, never ceases to create conditions which undermine it. Its self-inflicted wounds await our salt. If you don't believe in progress, it'll never disappoint you and you might even *make* some progress.

In some particulars, — as I've come to appreciate, somewhat to my surprise, in writing this essay, — traditional anarchist themes and practices are more attuned to popular predilections than ever before. Most Americans have joined them, for instance, in abstention from elections, and they just might be interested in the anarchists' reasons. Class conflict at the point of production holds little interest for campus-based Bookchinist-Arendtist civilogues, but means much to post-college workers reduced, for the duration, to the degradation they briefly thought they'd escaped by graduating from high school. Now they must work to pay off the loans that financed an interval of relative freedom (a Temporary Autonomous Zone, as it were) such as they may never enjoy again, no matter how much they earn. They may have learned just enough along the way to question whether life has to be this way.

But the new themes of the New Anarchism, or, better yet, the New Anarchisms also have popular appeal — not because they pander to prevalent illusions but because they pander (and why not?) to prevalent *dis*illusions. With technology, for instance. A *political* critique of technology may make a lot of sense to the tenders of high technology who have not experienced anything of its liberatory potential as so often promised but never delivered by the progressives, by the Marxists, syndicalists, Bookchinists and other technocrats. At the very least, trickle-down techno-liberation is as fraudulent as trickle-down enrichment through supply-side economics (make the already rich so much richer that some crumbs are bound to fall from their table). Computer programming is, if more interesting, little more liberatory than data entry, and the hours are longer. There's no light at the end of the carpal tunnel.

With whatever elements the New Anarchisms are compounded and whatever their fortunes will be, the old anarchism — the libertarian fringe of the Left That Was — is finished. The Bookchinist blip was a conjunctural quirk, an anomalous amalgam of the old anarchism and the New Left to which the Dean-to-be fortuitously added a little pop ecology and (this part passed unnoticed for far too long) his weird city-statist fetish. Now Bookchin belatedly bumbles forth as the defender of the faith, that old-time religion. Anarchism-as-Bookchinism was a confusionist episode even he, its fabricator, seems to be in haste to conclude.

If the word "decadence" means anything, *Social Anarchism or Lifestyle Anarchism* is an exercise in decadence, not to mention an exercise in futility. If the word means anything, it means a deterioration from a previous higher level of accomplishment — it means doing worse what was formerly done better. In that sense, the New Anarchisms of the "lifestyle anarchists" cannot be decadent, for what they are doing is at best, something better, and at worst, something different from what the old-style left-wing anarchists did. Bookchin is not even doing what Bookchin once did, if never very well, then at least a lot better.

Within anarchism, what is taking place resembles what, in science, is known as a paradigm shift (Kuhn 1970). A paradigm is an overarching frame of reference, something broader than a theory (or ideology), which directs the development of thought for those belonging to a community of those operating within the paradigm. That this is a somewhat circular formulation its originator admits (*ibid.:* 176), but truth *is* circular, an inescapable hermeneutic circle but one whose diameter we can widen along with our perspectives. The details and, for that matter, the deficiencies of Kuhn's much-discussed model of scientific theory and practice need not detain us here (although I commend them to anarchists capable of more muscular thinking than Bookchin and most other anarcho-eggheads are up for). Here I'm drawing attention to just two aspects of this historical approach to explaining theoretical thinking which I find suggestive.

The first is the notion of "normal science," which refers to the everyday practice of workaday scientists: the working-out of the implications of the prevailing paradigm. Newton's physics, for instance, kept observational astronomers and experimental physicists happy, or at least busy, for over two hundred years: it assigned them problems to solve and criteria for what counted as solutions to those problems.

The classical anarchism of Godwin, Proudhon, Bakunin and especially Kropotkin may be thought of as the original anarchist political paradigm. For all their differences, together they furnished many answers and a context for developing many more. Later figures like Malatesta, Goldman, Berkman, the anarcho-syndicalists, and the intellectuals writing for *Freedom* in effect engaged in "normal anarchism" — in restating, elaborating, updating and in details amending the paradigm. Men like Herbert Read, George Woodcock, Alex Comfort and Paul Goodman worked within this tradition in the inclement climate of the '40s and '50s. In characterizing their activity as derivative I am by no means denigrating it, or them. Precisely because the classical paradigm was rich in potential, intelligent anarchists have drawn fresh insights from it by applying it to changing 20th-century developments. But the developments have long since outstripped the paradigm. Too many "anomalies," as Kuhn calls them, have appeared to be reconciled with the paradigm without increasing strain and a deepening sense of artificiality. Classical anarchism, like leftism in general, is played out. Murray Bookchin, whom some anarchists once mistook for the first theorist of a new anarchist paradigm, has now come forth explicitly as the last champion of the old one, the anarchist tail of what he calls the Left That Was.

One other suggestive feature of Kuhn's argument is his account of how, on the ground, the supplanting of one paradigm by another actually takes place:

Bob Black

When, in the development of a natural science, an individual or group first produces a synthesis able to attract most of the *next generation's practitioners* [emphasis added], the older schools gradually disappear. In part their disappearance is caused by their members' conversion to the new paradigm. But there are always some men who cling to one or another of the older views, and they are simply read out of the profession, which thereafter ignores their work (Kuhn 1970: 18–19).

Kuhn goes on to explain that this may involve intransigent individuals, "more interesting, however, is the endurance of whole schools in increasing isolation from professional science. Consider, for example, the case of astrology, which was once an integral part of astronomy" (*ibid.:* 19 n. 11).

Not to pretend that anarchism is a science — such a pretense is itself a part of the obsolete paradigm — but the analogy is illuminating. As Bookchin admits, and deplores, "thousands" of anarchists, "the next generation's practitioners" of anarchism, are increasingly abandoning social anarchism for lifestyle anarchism. Some of the older school's practitioners convert, as has indeed happened. Other once-prominent figures, as Kuhn noticed (*ibid.),* marginalize themselves as the Dean has now done. And to clinch the comparison, what were once "integral parts" of anarchism are on the verge of splitting off on their own as did astrology from astronomy so as to have any hope of surviving at all. Bookchinism, "social ecology," was never an integral part of anarchism, for all the Dean's efforts to make it so. If it persists awhile after the Dean's demise, social ecology/anarchism will bear about the same relationship to the new anarchism as astrology to astronomy.

As will, I expect, the dwindling anarcho-leftist fundamentalisms. Of these there would seem to be only three. The first is the supposed pure-and-simple anarchism of, say, Fred Woodworth of *The Match!* or the late unlamented Bob Shea. The inherent improbability of a socially and economically agnostic anarchism — let's abolish the state and later sort out the trifling details, such as our way of life — as well as the sheer crackpotkinism of its vestigial devotees (Black 1994: 42–44) relegate this fundamentalism to imminent oblivion. Even

Bookchin would be embarrassed to be associated with it. A Marxist is capable of many errors and many horrors, and usually commits some, but one thing a Marxist cannot be indifferent to is political economy and the social relations of production.

The second obsolete anarcho-leftism is anarcho- syndicalism. Although it is a workerist ideology, its few working-class adherents are elderly. Although it is by definition a union-oriented ideology, there is no perceptible syndicalist presence in any union. A syndicalist is more likely to be a professor than a proletarian, more likely to be a folk singer than a factory worker. Organizers on principle, syndicalists are disunited and factionalized. Remarkably, this dullest of all anarchisms attracts some of the most irrational and hysterical adherents. Only a rather small minority of North American anarchists are syndicalists. Syndicalism will persist, if at all, as a campus-based cult in increasing isolation from the main currents of anarchism.

The third anarcho-leftism is anarcho-feminism. The category is, I admit, questionable. So-called radical feminism is leftist in origin but extreme right-wing in ideology (Black 1986: 133–138; Black 1992: 195–197). Separatist in tendency and sometimes in principle, anarcho-feminism is oriented much more toward statist feminism than anarchism. It is already well on its way toward encapsulation and isolation from the anarchisms. The feminist presence in anarchism is more apparent than real. Many anarchist women call themselves feminists from force of habit or because they think that by not so identifying themselves they somehow undermine those women who do. But there is little if anything distinctively feminist, fortunately, in the anarchism of most nominal anarcho-feminists. Feminism is so obviously an Establishment ideology and so remote from its (largely mythical) radical roots that its affirmation by anarchists will become ever more perfunctory. Like leftism, feminism is a needless liability for anarchists.

There is life after the left. And there is anarchy after anarchism. Post-leftist anarchists are striking off in many directions. Some may find the way — better yet, the ways — to a free future.

Bob Black, 1997

Bob Black

References

Adams, Robert M. (1983). *Decadent Societies.* San Francisco, CA: North Point Press

Adorno, Theodor W. (1990). "Punctuation Marks." *The Antioch Review* (Summer): 300–305

Andrieux, Maurice (1972). *Daily Life in Venice in the Time of Casanova.* New York & Washington, DC: Praeger Publisher

[Anonymous] (1988). Review of *The Rise of Urbanization and the Decline of Citizenship,* by Murray Bookchin. *Orbis: A Journal of World Affairs* 32 (Fall): 628

[Anonymous] (1996). Review of *Social Anarchism or Lifestyle Anarchism: An Unbridgeable Chasm,* by Murray Bookchin. *Green Anarchist* 42 (Summer): 22–23

Ansell-Pearson, Keith (1994).*An Introduction to Nietzsche as Political Thinker: The Perfect Nihilist.* Cambridge: Cambridge University Press

Apter, David E., & James Joll, eds. (1972). *Anarchism Today.* Garden City, NY: Anchor Books

Arendt, Hannah (1958). *The Human Condition.* Chicago, IL & London: University of Chicago Press

Avrich, Paul (1984). *The Haymarket Tragedy.* Princeton, NJ: Princeton University Press

Babbie, Earl (1992). *The Practice of Social Research.* Sixth Edition. Belmont, CA: Wadsworth Publishing Company

Bailyn, Bernard (1992). *The Ideological Origins of the American Revolution.* Enlarged Edition. Cambridge: Harvard University Press

Bakunin, Michael (1990). *Statism and Anarchy.* Edited by Marshall Shatz. Cambridge: Cambridge University Press

Bob Black

Beals, Ralph L. (1969). *Politics of Social Research: An Inquiry into the Ethics and Responsibilities of Social Scientists.* Chicago, IL: Aldine Publishing Company

Benbow, William (n.d.). *Grand National Holiday and Congress of the Productive Classes.* Edited by SA. Bushell. London: Pelagian Press

Bey, Hakim (1991). *T.A.Z.: The Temporary Autonomous Zone, Ontological Anarchism, Poetic Terrorism.* Brooklyn, NY: Autonomedia

Binford, Lewis R., & W.J. Chasto, Jr. (1976). "Nunamiut Demographic History: A Provocative Case." In Zubrow (1976), pp. 63–143

Binford, Sally R. (1968). "Ethnographic Data and Understanding the Pleistocene." In Lee & DeVore (1968a), pp. 274–275

Black, Bob (1986). *The Abolition of Work and Other Essays.* Port Townsend, WA: Loompanics Unlimited

— (1992). *Friendly Fire.* Brooklyn, NY: Autonomedia

— (1994). *Beneath the Underground.* Portland, OR: Feral House

— (1996a). "Technophilia, An Infantile Disorder." *Green Anarchist* 42 (Summer): 13–15

— (1996b). "What's Wrong With This Picture?" *Exquisite Corpse* 57: 43–45

— (1996c). Unpublished review of *Grand National Holiday and Congress of the Productive Classes*, by William Benbow

— (1996d). "Zero Work." *Small Magazine Review* 28(6) (June): 22

— , & Mike Gunderloy (1992). "Neo-Individualism Reconsidered." In Black (1992), pp. 199–201

— , & Adam Parfrey, eds. (1989). *Rants and Incendiary Tracts: Voices of Desperate Illumination, 1558 to Present.* New York: Amok Press & Port Townsend, WA: Loompanics Unlimited

Black, Robert C. [Bob Black] (1985). "The Heavenly City of the 20th-Century Political Philosopher: Walzer on Judging." *Legal Studies Forum* 9(3): 259–279

Blainey, Geoffrey (1976). *Triumph of the Nomads: A History of Aboriginal Australia.* Woodstock, NY: Overlook Press

Bolloten, Burnett (1991). *The Spanish Civil War.* Chapel Hill, NC: University of North Carolina Press

Bookchin, Murray (1970). "The Youth Culture: An Anarcho-Communist View." In *Hip Culture: Six Essays on Its Revolutionary Potential* (New York: Times Change Press), pp. 51–63

— (1971). *Post-Scarcity Anarchism.* Berkeley, CA: The Ramparts Press

— (1974). *The Limits of the City.* New York: Harper & Row Colophon Books

— (1977). *The Spanish Anarchists: The Heroic Years, 1868–1936.* New York: Free Life Editions, 1977

— (1979). "Marxism as Bourgeois Sociology." *Our Generation* 13(3) (Summer): 21–28

— (1982). *The Ecology of Freedom: The Emergence and Dissolution of Hierarchy.* Palo Alto, CA: Cheshire Books

— (1987a). *The Rise of Urbanization and the Decline of Citizenship.* San Francisco, CA: Sierra Club Books

— (1987b). "Thinking Ecologically: A Dialectical Approach." 18(2) *Our Generation* (March): 3–40

Bob Black

— (1989). *Remaking Society.* Montreal, Canada & New York: Black Rose Books

— (1990). "Radical Politics in an Era of Advanced Capitalism." *Our Generation* 21(2) (June): 1–12

— (1991). *Ecology of Freedom: The Emergence and Dissolution of Hierarchy.* Revised Edition. Montreal, Canada: Black Rose Books

— (1994). *To Remember Spain: The Anarchist and Syndicalist Revolution of 1936.* Edinburgh, Scotland & San Francisco, CA: AK Press

— (1996). "Anarchism: Past and Present." In Ehrlich (1996), pp. 19–30

Boyd, Robert, & Peter J. Richerson (1993). "Culture and Human Evolution." In Rasmussen (1993), pp. 119–134

Borkenau, Franz (1963). *The Spanish Cockpit.* Ann Arbor, MI: University of Michigan Press, Ann Arbor Paperbacks

Brademas, Stephen John (1953). "Revolution and Social Revolution: A Contribution to the History of the Anarcho-Syndicalist Movement in Spain: 1930–1937." Ph.D dissertation, University of Oxford

Bradford, George (1996). "Media: Capital's Global Village." In Ehrlich (1996), pp. 258–271

Broué, Pierre, & Émile Témime (1972). *The Revolution and the Civil War in Spain.* Cambridge: MIT Press

Brown, L. Susan (1993). *The Politics of Individualism: Liberalism, Liberal Feminism and Anarchism.* Montreal, Canada: Black Rose Books

— (1995). "Does Work Really Work?" *Kick It Over* 35: 14- 17

Camatte, Jacques (1995). *This World We Must Leave and Other Essays* . Edited by Alex Trotter. Brooklyn, NY: Autonomedia

Clark, John (1982). Review of *Toward an Ecological Society,* by Murray Bookchin. *Our Generation* 18(2) (Summer): 52–59

— (1984). *The Anarchist Moment: Reflections on Culture, Nature and Power.* Montreal, Canada: Black Rose Books

— (1990). "Bookchin, Murray (b. 1921)." *Encyclopedia of the American Left,* ed. Mari Jo Buhle, Paul Buhle & Dan Georgakas. New York & London: Garland Publications

Cohen, Mark N. (1987). "The Significance of Long-Term Changes in Human Diet and Food Economy." In Harris & Ross (1987), pp. 261–283

Cohen, M.N., & G.S. Armelagos, eds. (1984). *Paleopathology at the Dawn of Agriculture.* New York: Academic Press

Colbourn, H. Trevor (1965). *The Lamp of Experience: Whig History and the Intellectual Origins of the American Revolution.* Chapel Hill, NC: University of North Carolina Press

Conkey, Margaret W. (1984). "To Find Ourselves: Art and Social Geography of Prehistoric Hunter Gatherers." In Schrere (1984), pp. 253–276

Cooke, Jacob E., ed. (1961). *The Federalist.* Middletown, CT: Wesleyan University Press

Cowan, Ruth Schwartz (1974). "A Case Study of Technological Change: The Washing Machine and the Working Wife." In Hartman & Banner (1974), pp. 245–253

— (1983). *More Work for Mother: The Irony of Household Technology from the Open Hearth to the Microwave.* New York: Basic Books

Dahl, Robert A. (1990). *After the Revolution: Authority in a Good Society.* Revised Edition. New Haven, CT & London: Yale University Press

Bob Black

Damas, David, ed. (1969). *Contributions to Anthropology: Band Societies.* Ottawa, Canada: National Museum of Canada

De Leon, David (1978). *The American as Anarchist: Reflections on Indigenous Radicalism.* Baltimore, MD & London: The Johns Hopkins University Press

— (1996). "For Democracy Where We Work: A Rationale for Self-Management" In Ehrlich (1996), pp. 192–210

Denbow, James R. (1984). "Prehistoric Herders and Foragers of the Kalahari: The Evidence for 1500 Years of Interaction." In Schrire (1984), pp. 175–193

Denevan, William (1992). "The Pristine Myth: The Landscape of the Americas in *1492" Annals of the Association of American Geographers* 82: 369–385

Dunn, Frederick L. (1968). "Epidemological Factors: Health and Disease in Hunter-Gatherers." In Lee & DeVore (1968a), pp. 221–228

Eckersley, Robyn (1989). "Divining Evolution: The Ecological Ethics of Murray Bookchin." *Environmental Ethics* 11(2) (Summer): 99–116

Ehrlich, Howard J., ed. (1996). *Reinventing Anarchy, Again.* Edinburgh, Scotland & San Francisco, CA: AK Press

Feyerabend, Paul (1975). *Against Method: Outline of an Anarchistic Theory of Knowledge.* London: NLB & Atlantic Highlands, NJ: Humanities Press

— (1987). *Farewell to Reason.* London & New York: Verso

Finlay, M.I. (1959). "Was Greek Civilisation Based on Slave Labour?" *Historia* 8: 145–164

— (1985). *Democracy Ancient and Modern.* Second Edition. London: The Hogarth Press

Flint, R.W., ed. (1972). *Marinetti: Selected Writings.* New York: Farrer, Straus & Giroux

For Ourselves (1983). *The Right to Be Greedy: Theses on the Practical Necessity of Demanding Everything.* Port Townsend, WA: Loompanics Unlimited

Fraser, Ronald (1979). *Blood of Spain: An Oral History of the Spanish Civil War.* New York: Pantheon

Gilman, Richard (1975). *Decadence.* New York: Farrer, Straus & Giroux

Goddard College (1995). *1995 Off-Campus Catalog.* Plainfield, VT: Goddard College

— (1996). *Addendum to Off Campus Catalog.* Plainfield, VT: Goddard College

Goodman, Paul (1994). *Crazy Hope and Finite Experience: Final Essays of Paul Goodman.* Edited by Taylor Stoehr. San Francisco, CA: Jossey-Bass, Inc.

— , & Percival Goodman (1960). *Communitas: Means of Livelihood and Ways of Life.* Second Edition, Revised. New York: Vintage Books

Gordon, Robert J. (1984). "The !Kung in the Kalahari Exchange: An Ethnohistorical Perspective." In Schrire (1984), pp. 195–224

Gregg, Susan, ed. (1991). *Between Bands and States.* Carbondale, IL: Southern University of Illinois at Carbondale

Harris, Marvin, & Eric B. Ross, eds. (1987). *Food and Evolution: Toward a Theory of Human Food Habits.* Philadelphia, PA: Temple University Press

Hart, John M. (1978). *Anarchism and the Mexican Working Class, 1860–1931.* Austin, TX & London: U. of Texas Press

Bob Black

Hartman, Mary S., & Lois Banner, eds. (1974). *Clio's Consciousness Raised: New Perspectives on the History of Women.* New York: Harper & Row

Hastrup, Kirsten, & Peter Hervik, eds. (1994). *Social Experience and Anthropological Knowledge.* New York: Routledge

Hawkes, Kristen (1987). "How Much Food Do Foragers Need?" In Harris & Ross (1987), pp. 341–355

Herber, Lewis [Murray Bookchin] (1963). *Our Synthetic Environment*

— [Murray Bookchin] (1965). *Crisis in Our Cities.* Englewood Cliffs, N.J.: Prentice-Hall

Holton, Gerald (1993). *Science and Anti-Science.* Cambridge: Harvard University Press

Hughes, H. Stuart (1961). *Consciousness and Society: The Reorientation of European Social Thought, 1890–1930.* New York: Alfred A. Knopf

Hunnicutt, Benjamin Kline (1988). *Work Without End: Abandoning Shorter Hours for the Right to Work.* Philadelphia, PA: Temple University Press

Illich, Ivan (1981). *Shadow Work.* Boston, MA: Marion Boyars

Institute for Social Ecology (1996). *1996 Catalog.* Plainfield, VT: Institute for Social Ecology

Jarach, Lawrence (1996). "Manichean Anarchism or Dishonest Anarchism; Judging a Bookchin by His Cover-Ups." Unpublished review of *Social Anarchism or Lifestyle Anarchism* forthcoming in *Anarchy: A Journal of Desire Aimed*

Kelly, Robert C. (1991). "Sedantism, Sociopolitical Inequality, and Resource Fluctuations." In Gregg (1991), pp. 135–158

Knauft, Bruce M. (1987). "Divergence Between Cultural Success and Reproductive Success in Preindustrial Cities." *Cultural Anthropology* 2(1) (Feb.): 94–114

Konner, Melvin, & Marjorie Shostak (1987). "Timing and Management of Birth Among the !Kung: Biocultural Interaction in Reproductive Adaptation." *Cultural Anthropology* 2(1) (Feb.): 11–28

Kropotkin, Pierre (1890). *The Place of Anarchism in Socialistic Evolution.* London: William Reeves

Kropotkin, Peter (1947). *Ethics: Origin and Development.* New York: The Dial Press

— (1990). "Preface" to *How We Shall Bring About the Revolution: Syndicalism and the Cooperative Commonwealth,* by Emile Pataud and Emile Pouget. In Pataud & Pouget (1990), pp. xxxi-xxxvii

— (1995). *The Conquest of Bread and Other Writings.* Edited by Marshall S. Shatz. Cambridge: Cambridge University Press

Kuhn, Thomas S. (1970). *The Structure of Scientific Revolutions.* Second Edition, Enlarged. Chicago, IL: University of Chicago Press

Lasswell, Harold (1958). *Politics: Who Gets What, When, How.* With Postscript. New York: Meridian Books

Lee, Richard Borshay (1968). "What Hunters Do for a Living, or, How to Make Out on Scarce Resources." In Lee & Devore (1968), pp. 30–48

— (1969). "!Kung Bushmen Subsistence: An Input-Output Analysis." In Vayda (1969), pp. 47–79

— (1979). *The !Kung San: Men, Women and Work in a Foraging Society.* Cambridge: Cambridge University Press

— , & Irven DeVore, eds. (1968a). *Man the Hunter.* Chicago: Aldine Publishing Company

Bob Black

— & Irven DeVore (1968b). "Preface." in Lee & DeVore (1968a), pp. vii-ix

— , & Irven DeVore (1968c). "Problems in the Study of Hunters and Gatherers." In Lee & DeVore (1968a), pp. 3–12

Legge, Anthony J., & Peter A. Rowley-Conwy (1987). "Gazelle Killing in Stone Age Syria." *Scientific American* 257(2) (August): 88–95

Lenin, V.I. (1940). *"Left-Wing" Communism, an Infantile Disorder: A Popular Essay in Marxian Strategy and Tactics.* (Little Lenin Library, Vol. 20.) N.Y.: International Publishers

— (1950). *Materialism and Empirio-Criticism: Critical Comments on a Reactionary Philosophy.* London: Lawrence and Wishart Ltd.

Lévi-Strauss, Claude (1962). *The Savage Mind.* Chicago, IL: University of Chicago Press & London: Weidenfeld and Nicholson

Lowie, Robert H. (1963). *Indians of the Plains.* Garden City, NY: The Natural History Press

Marx, Karl (1967). *Capital: A Critique of Political Economy.* Edited by Frederick Engels. Vol. III: *The Process of Capitalist Production as a Whole.* New York: International Publishers

McCusker, John J., & Russell R. Menard (1985). *The Economy of British America, 1607–1789.* Chapel Hill, NC & London: University of North Carolina Press

Megill, Allan, ed. (1994). *Rethinking Objectivity.* Durham, NC: University of North Carolina Press

Michels, Robert (1962). *Political Parties: A Sociological Study of the Oligarchical Tendencies of Modern Democracy.* New York: The Free Press

Monegal, Emir Rodriguez, & Alastair Reid, eds. (1981). *Borges: A Reader.* New York: E.P. Dutton

Moore, John (1996). "Commentary on the Anarcho-Futurist Manifesto." *Green Anarchist* 40/41 (Spring): 18–20

Morgan, Edmund S. (1975). *American Slavery, American Freedom: The Ordeal of Colonial Virginia.* New York & London: W.W. Norton & Company

Murdoek, George Peter (1968). "The Current Status of the World's Hunting and Gathering Peoples." In Lee & DeVore (1968a), pp. 13–20

Newcomb, W.W., Jr. (1961). *The Indians of Texas.* Austin, TX: University of Texas Press

Nietzsche, Friedrich (1994). *On the Genealogy of Morality.* Edited by Keith Ansell-Pearson. Cambridge: Cambridge University Press

Novatore, Renzo (1989). "Iconoclasts, Forward!" In Black & Parfrey (1989), pp. 92–93

Novick, Peter (1988). *That Noble Dream: The "Objectivity Question" and the American Historical Profession.* Cambridge: Cambridge University Press

Nuquist, Andrew E. (1964). *Town Government in Vermont.* Burlington, VT: University of Vermont Government Research Center

Orwell, George (1952). *Homage to Catalonia.* New York & London: Harcourt Brace Jovanovich

Pannekoek, Anton (1948). *Lenin as Philosopher: A Critical Examination of the Philosophical Basis of Leninism.* New York: New Essays

Parkington, John E. (1984). "Soaqua and Bushmen: Hunters and Robbers." In Schrire (1984), pp. 151–174

Pataud, Emile, & Emile Pouget (1990). *How We Shall Bring About the Revolution: Syndicalism and the Cooperative Commonwealth.* London & Winchester, MA: Pluto Press

Bob Black

Peters, Pauline (1990). "The San Historicized." *Science* 248 (May 28): 905–907

Popper, Karl L. (1962). *The Open Society and Its Enemies.* 2 vols. Fourth Edition, Revised. New York & Evanston, IL: Harper Torchbooks

Proudhon, P.-J. (1979). *The Principle of Federation.* Edited by Richard Vernon. Toronto, Canada: University of Toronto Press

Rasmussen, D. Tab, ed. (1993). *The Origin and Evolution of Humans and Humanness.* Boston, MA & London: Jones and Bartlett Publisher

Renouf, MA.P. (1991). "Sedentary Hunter-Gathers: A Case for Northern Coasts." In Gregg (1991), pp. 89–107

Richards, Vernon (1983). *Lessons of the Spanish Revolution, 1936–1939.* Revised, Enlarged Edition. London: Freedom Press

Rifkin, Jeremy (1995). *The End of Work: The Decline of the Global Labor Force and the Dawn of the Post-Market Era.* New York: G.P. Putnam's Sons

Roberts, David D. (1979). *The Syndicalist Tradition and Italian Fascism.* Chapel Hill, NC: University of North Carolina Press

Rocker, Rudolf (1947). *Anarcho-syndicalism: Vieory and Practice.* Indore, India: Modern Publishers

Ross, Eric B. (1987). "An Overview of Trends in Dietary Variation from Hunter-Gatherer to Modern Capitalist Societies." In Harris & Ross (1987), pp. 7–55

Ruby, Jay (1996). "Objectivity Revisited." *American Anthropologist* 98(2) (June): 398–400

Ruhart, Mary (1996). "Keeping Our Freedom in an Unfree World." *Formulations* 3(3) (Spring): 3–4, 13

Sahlins, Marshall (1972). *Stone Age Economics.* Chicago, IL: Aldine Publishing Company

Salisbury, Neal (1982). *Manitou and Providence: Indians, Europeans, and the Making of New England, 1500–1643.* New York & Oxford: Oxford University Press

Scheiber, Harry N., Harold G. Vatter & Harold Underwood Faulkner (1976). *American Economic History.* New York: Harper & Row

Schor, Juliet (1991). *The Overworked American: The Unexpected Decline of Leisure.* New York: Basic Books

Schrire, Carmel, ed. (1984). *Past and Present in Hunter Gatherer Societies.* Orlando, FL: Academic Press

Schuster, Eunice Minette (1932). *Native American Anarchism: A Study of Left-Wing American Individualism.* (Smith College Studies in History, Vol. XVII, Nos. 1–4.) Northampton, MA: Smith College Department of History

Seidman, Michael (1991). *Workers Against Work: Labor in Paris and Barcelona During the Popular Fronts.* Berkeley: University of California Press

Sender, Ramón J. (1990). *Seven Red Sundays.* Chicago, IL: Ivan R. Dee, Publisher

Silbener, Edmund (1948). "Proudhon's Judeophobia." *Historica Judaica* 11(1) (April): 61–80

Sjoberg, Gideon (1960). *The Preindustrial City: Past and Present.* Glencoe, IL: The Free Press

Smith, Gregory B. (1983). Review of *The Ecology of Freedom,* by Murray Bookchin. *American Political Science Review* 77(1) (March): 540

Bob Black

Solway, Jacqueline S., & Richard B. Lee (1990). "Foragers, Genuine or Spurious? Situating the Kalahari San in History." *Current Anthropology* 31(2) (April): 109–146

Stafford, David (1972). "Anarchists in Britain Today." In Apter & Joll (1972), pp. 99–122

Stirner, Max (1978). "Stirner's Critics." *Philosophical Forum* 8(2–4): 66–80

— (1995). *The Ego and Its Own.* Edited by David Leopold. Cambridge: Cambridge University Press

Tanaka, Jiri (1980). *The San Hunter-Gatherers of the Kalahari: A Study in Ecological Anthropology.* Tokyo, Japan: University of Tokyo Press

Thissen, Siebe (1996). *De Weg naar Croatan.* (De Kunst van het Afhaken.) Rotterdam, Netherlands: Baalprodukties Sittard

Tocqueville, Alexis de (1969a). *Democracy in America.* Edited by J.P. Mayer. Garden City, New York: Anchor Books

— (1969b). "Report Given Before the Academy of Moral and Political Sciences on January 15, 1848, on the Subject of M. Cherbuliez' Book Entitled *On Democracy in Switzerland.*" In Tocqueville (1969a), pp. 736–749 (Appendix II)

Tuchman, Barbara (1966). *The Proud Tower.* New York: The Macmillan Company

Vayda, Andrew P., ed. (1969). *Environment and Cultural Behavior.* New York: Natural History Press

Vincent, K. Steven (1984). *Pierre-Joseph Proudhon and the Rise of French Republican Socialism.* Oxford: Oxford University Press

Walter, Nicolas (1972). "Anarchism in Print: Yesterday and Today." In Apter & Joll (1972), pp. 147–168

Walzer, Michael (1970). *Obligations: Essays on Disobedience, War, and Citizenship.* Cambridge: Harvard University Press

Watson, Richard A. (1995). Review of *Which Way for the Ecology Movement?* by Murray Bookchin. *Environmental Ethics* 14(4) (Winter): 437–439

Wilmsen, Edwin N. (1989). *Land Filled with Flies: A Political Economy of the Kalahari.* Chicago, IL & London: University of Chicago Press

Woodburn, J. (1982). "Egalitarian Societies." *Man* 7: 431–451

Woodcock, George (1962). *Anarchism: A History of Libertarian Ideas and Movements.* New York: Meridian Books

Yengoyan, Aram A. (1968). "Demographic and Ecological Influences on Aboriginal Australian Marriage Sections." In Lee & DeVore (1968), pp. 185–199

Zapatistas (1994). *Zapatistas! Documents of the New Mexican Revolution.* Brooklyn, NY: Autonomedia

Zerzan, John (1987). *Elements of Refusal.* Seattle, WA: Left Bank Books

— (1994). *Future Primitive and Other Essays.* Brooklyn, NY: Autonomedia & Columbia, MO: Anarchy/C.A.L. Press

— (1996). Letter to Bob Black, May 20

Zimmern, Alfred (1931). *The Greek Commonwealth: Politics and Economics in Fifth-Century Athens.* Fifth Edition, Revised. Oxford: at the Clarendon Press

Zubrow, Ezra B.W., ed. (1976). *Demographic Anthropology: Quantitative Approaches.* Albuquerque, NM: University of New Mexico Press

Bob Black

APPENDIX

Bob Black

WHAT LEFT AND RIGHT REALLY MEAN

Invocations of 'Left' and 'Right' are extremely common in political discussions. Typically, they are deployed as hopelessly vague terms of abuse or goofy indications of team loyalty, unfortunately including among anarchists, libertarians, and other radicals.

I have argued for years that these terms are so broad and multifarious in their usage that they have been bleached of almost any meaning and should be abandoned by sensible people interested in coherent dialogue in favor of a multi-dimensional political grid. Naturally, this objection is rarely heard, and I am often nonetheless pressed to answer where I stand on Left versus Right.

My usual response is to say that the Left versus Right spectrum is not merely accidentally incoherent, but *deliberately* so, in that its constant usage in mainstream discourse is a form of *divide et impera* by the power elite that is simply the next level up from the Democrat versus Republican binary. Many people recognize the latter as a bullshit choice, but nonetheless maintain that Left versus Right is a real and natural split – in my view, it is instead meant to get the politically active masses to play team sports that the power elite can regulate and broker, making all of the Little People compete with, direct invective at, and even physically assault *one another* rather than their wise overlords. *Divide et impera* is the oldest power game the elite have, and it has worked extremely well for millennia.

If I am pressed further, perhaps with a "Yes, that's fine and well, but we all know there are real differences among these people all the same – they aren't fighting over *nothing*, even if they are encouraged to fight." There are indeed differences, but why should those be mapped with a division based on 18th-century French politics? The etymology of Left and Right is *literally* a reference to the French Revolution, during which attendees of the National Assembly gathered to the right of the president to indicate their support for the *ancien regime*, while those on the president's left indicated their support of the Revolution. Is there really anything consistent in these groupings from that very specific time and place to today, anywhere on the planet where these terms are used?

Perhaps, but it is not usually what it is said to be. It is sometimes said (even on Wikipedia today, which can be taken as an indication of pseudo-democratic, establishment consensus opinion) that being on the Left is about valuing egalitarianism, while the Right necessarily values one or more forms of hierarchy that are seen as legitimate. This is sometimes true but ultimately points at changeable surface qualities rather than fundamentals – and it is hence easy to find counterexamples: the various State Communist regimes of the 20th and 21st centuries were or are assuredly 'Left' in some broad form, yet it would be ridiculous to claim that these did or do not possess crushing, parasitic hierarchies. And the various strands of Right-libertarianism or Right-anarchism are far less hierarchical than almost all forms of Leftism, even if they almost always maintain the legitimacy of meritocratic "natural elites" (Hoppe) or certain more or less voluntary or organic traditional hierarchical structures like the family or religious organizations.

Another frequent false claim is that the Left/Right spectrum really measures the ineradicable tension between equality and liberty. There are again immediately apparent problems with this notion, the most obvious being that, while certainly sometimes in tension, equality and liberty are not necessarily *always* at odds with one another: the cancerous growth of a State on a human population tends to decrease *both* equality *and* liberty, as it produces a rapacious power elite who hoard wealth to enrich themselves while removing civil liberties to squelch dissidents. Secondly, just as the Left is not *ultimately* but only *circumstantially* about politico-economic equality, so it is the case with the Right and liberty. Many moderate conservatives in the modern West are willing to legislate against personal liberties in favor of protecting traditional moral values. And the Fascist regimes of the 20th century enormously subordinated individual liberty to State and Nation (it is sometimes argued that Fascism is actually an oddball offshoot of Marxism and therefore more appropriately placed on the Left – I think this contention has considerable merit, but in my view it is best to consider Fascism a

Left/Right hybrid and thus still exemplary of certain Rightist values. I will write more on this in the future).

If we grant that this distinction has any meaning, then, what is it? Having dismissed the above politico-ethical distinctions, I believe we can now show that the real differences between Left and Right, and the reason that people tend to group themselves in these camps across widely differing times and places, is the disagreements are not in political or ethical views *per se*, but in *ontological and metaphysical* views. These differences are at least three-fold.

The first and second differences concern questions of human nature. The paleoconservative scholar Paul Gottfried has suggested – correctly, in my view – that a core tenet of Leftism, whether held consciously or not by any given adherent, is that the differences we observe among human beings (in abilities, in quality of life outcomes, in beliefs, etc.) are primarily (or even, at the outer limits of Leftist ideology, *entirely*) the result of social and environmental conditioning rather than inborn constitution of some kind. Right-wingers, correspondingly, tend to believe that the inborn character of people (be it conceived of in material, spiritual, volitional, or other terms) matters more in whom they ultimately become. This elegantly simple observation of Gottfried's is sufficient to explain how vastly different views like an anarcho-capitalism that wants to abolish all States and a Neo-Reactionism that wants to restore hereditary monarchies are both recognizably 'Right-wing' – one justifies difference on nothing but merit, the other on royal blood or divine right, but both believe different people are entitled to different social outcomes *because difference is real, natural, and just*. Gottfried's point also helps to illuminate, as another example, why so many Left-wing people, no matter how much they may disagree with each other about political or economic questions, will unite in being averse to the concept of heritable IQ, since it suggests the existence of potentially ineradicable, socially important, and objectively measurable natural differences in ability.

The second question of human nature, related to but nonetheless separate from the first, is what the Chicago School economist Thomas

Bob Black

Sowell called the "constrained" versus "unconstrained" visions of humanity, which he outlined in detail in his 1987 book *A Conflict of Visions*. The "unconstrained" vision is utopian, believes in the essential good of humanity, and strives for the perfectibility of the human creature and the social order. Thus, Rousseau believed man was born free but chained by society, the Soviet ideologues postulated the coming of the morally perfect "New Soviet Man", and John Zerzan maintains we need only throw off all domestication in order to arrive at an Edenic communion with nature and one another that is our natural birthright. Conversely, the "constrained" vision is essentially tragic, views the human as a fallen creature who irremediably tends toward corruption, and believes society can never be perfected, but only carefully steered to keep the worst at bay. Thus, Hobbes referenced the Roman proverb *homo homini lupus* ("Man is wolf to man") in describing human attitudes toward strangers and foreigners, René Guénon lamented that all of the efforts of 'progress' in technology and democratization were Icarian misadventures, and Murray Rothbard excoriated the legitimacy of the State primarily in terms of moral hypocrisy relative to natural law. The widely divergent conclusions of these thinkers are rooted in a common premise on a single issue.

The third and final difference, I will contend, is purely metaphysical and often unarticulated. Consciously or not, every person has to answer essential questions that implicitly undergird the answers to all more derivative questions: What is the relationship between the human mind and the world it seems to encounter? Are the boundaries between ideas clear and objective, or are they fuzzy and indeterminate? Do transcendental entities inform the world, or are we making it up as we go?

Roughly speaking, one can be a *realist* or a *subjectivist* on a number of core issues. On the one hand, we have moral realism, a teleological Nature, a Platonic view of concepts as actually-existing things, and an epistemic optimism that sees human beings as essentially capable of knowing the world. And, on the other hand, we have moral relativism or nihilism of some kind, a belief in Nature as aimless and accidental, an instrumental view of concepts as personal or social constructs, and an epistemological skepticism that doubts whether so-called knowledge is more than a set of pragmatic fictions. Again, roughly speaking, we have a Traditional metaphysical view on the one end, a Modernist view in the middle, and a Postmodern or nihilistic view at the other extreme.

As an aside, it is worth noting in case it is not obvious that none of the above are fully binary choices. We thus have phenomena like the famous (but frankly rather dull) Chomsky-Foucault debate in which two Leftists' argument turned on the fact that Chomsky was a moral realist and an essentialist about certain aspects of human nature, whereas Foucault indulged in the nihilistic epistemic and moral conclusions of postmodern deconstructionism. And of course there are hybrid characters like Renzo Novatore, who very obviously had an unconstrained Rousseauvian desire to destroy all social chains as quickly as possible, but who also maintained a Nietzschean personal elitism that scorned the avolitional slavishness of the NPCs of his day, be they bourgeois or proletarian.

It has been a personal irony for me, as someone who considered himself to be on the far-Left beginning as a teenager, to have realized in the past few years that I actually come down decidedly on the Right on all three of these questions. This three-fold schema also helped me to understand why the 'Post-Left' tendency in anarchism, in spite of breaking with anarcho-leftism on so many ethical and strategic questions, nonetheless has a dyed-in-the-wool leftism about it when it comes to certain questions.

Bellamy Fitzpatrick, 2019

Bob Black